THE HOT TENT

DIARIES

JOHN D BURNS

The Hot Tent Diaries

John D Burns

First published 2022 by John D. Burns

ISBN 978-0-9955958-6-6

Also by John D. Burns

The Last Hillwalker
Bothy Tales
Sky Dance
Wild Winter

Contents

Come softly and treasure this land, for it is here that
you belong. Touch the ground only with your
fingertips and the hills with your eyes, so those who
come after will know your heart is here.

Exploring Scotland in a Hot Tent
Book 1

Starlight and Smoke

Introduction

Beyond the canvas walls of my tent there is nothing between me and the vast starlit sky. Around me, the hills sweep up steeply from the depths of the glen. Beneath the night sky all is steeped in a darkness so profound you could touch it. The glow from my tent is the only island of light in this dark sea. I never expected to be here, bathing in the heat from my wood-burning stove, my feet resting on thick carpet. Occasionally, the flame in the polished-brass lamp flickers and reminds me of the bothies I used to spend nights like these in. Sometimes roads lead to unexpected places and I'm grateful that this one took me here.

I have been exploring the Highlands, using basic shelters known as bothies, for many years. My passion for these crude places has become the centre of my life. If you have never visited a bothy, then I had better explain. They are open cottages, lacking any facilities other than shelter from the elements and a roof to sleep under. They have no running water, electricity or plumbing. The only heating comes from any coal you carry in and the only lighting from your candles.

To enjoy a night in a bothy it helps to be an incurable romantic. Sat before a bothy fire on a lonely night, with the wind battering against the walls and the candles flickering, my imagination wanders. I return to a simpler time; a time when being dry and warm and having enough to eat was all it took to be happy. A bothy night is like spending an evening in the fifteenth century –hopefully without the fleas and the ever-present danger of a violent death, although one can never be certain. Most weeks I would spend a few nights in one of these remote shelters. Sometimes I'd be alone, while at other times I'd enjoy the company of a few like-minded souls.

I thought that's how I'd spend the days of my retirement: happily bothy-hopping and time-travelling into my dotage or at least until my knees gave out. However, fate, or rather a worldwide pandemic, changed all that. In 2020 the Covid-19 pandemic closed bothies and it was months before any of us could go anywhere at all. When travel restrictions eased, I had nowhere to go. My nights of solitude in wild and remote, silent places were at an end until I remembered –I had a tent!

I made plans. I would retrieve my lightweight two-man tent from the back of the cupboard where it had sat for a number of years and head off into the hills. Fond memories returned to me of long walks into remote corries during the adventures of my youth. I could see myself once again relaxing in my tent, leaving the hubbub of everyday life far behind. Never mind that bothies were closed –I would stride out with my tent, off into the sunset, beyond the next horizon. At least, that was the idea.

Lightweight backpacking tents give unparalleled freedom. My first few backpacking expeditions with my two-man tent as a bothy-substitute quickly reminded me of some of the things that I had forgotten about lightweight tents. They reminded me that I am now in my late sixties and struggle to perform some of the gymnastics required for a small tent. Trying to put my trousers on in the morning meant a twenty-minute horizontal limbo dance that left me sweating and exhausted. I would find myself struggling into the wrong trouser leg or putting my foot into a pocket. When I tried to find a comfortable position to sit and read or to watch something on my phone, one shoulder would go numb; I'd transfer to the other shoulder and the feeling in that shoulder would soon depart also. I would spend an hour or so shoulder-shuffling, so I would give up and retreat into the depths of my sleeping bag. I had forgotten that winter nights in the Highlands in a small tent are long and cold.

I needed a bigger tent, I decided —one that I could sit upright in and spend my nights in comfort, and which would allow an older gentleman such as myself to stand up when he put his trousers on. No more of that damned wriggling for me. I bought a bigger bell tent, with a single pole, that was big enough for me to stand up in but not so big I couldn't keep it warm using a paraffin lamp or two. As soon as I erected it on my first wild camp in the north, I realised it was far too light to be able to withstand the Sutherland weather. The wind entertained itself that afternoon by tossing my new tent around as though it were a child's toy. As I cooked my tea, I hung on to the central pole like a sailor clinging on to the mast of his sinking ship. By Sutherland standards I knew this was just a breeze. This tent would never cope with the winds of winter. I needed a heavier tent, and my next step was to get a traditional family tent; the sort with two bedrooms and a kitchen area, with room for two kids and a dog, complete with windows and curtains. A nylon suburbia.

I decided to erect my second tent on a west coast campsite. At least if the weather got too much, I'd have some toilets to shelter in. The weather on the west coast of Scotland rarely disappoints and I found myself in a wrestling match with my new tent as the wind desperately tried to hurl the mass of canvas into the sea, rain saturating both the tent and me. At last, I won the fight with three falls and a submission, and my family tent was up. At least inside I was out of the rain and able to get into dry clothes. This tent did better than its lighter predecessor; it remained firmly in place. I settled down amongst the caravans and mobile homes, with my Tilley lamp purring away. It was better than my last attempt but even now the wind battered against the walls and found its way inside the tent. This was only September, but it was chilly enough to tell me that keeping warm in a tent like this in December in the Highlands would be impossible. That night I tried to reconcile myself to the fact that perhaps I would be unable to find a tent that would allow me to have the freedom I had once enjoyed in my bothy ramblings.

The following morning I awoke in a grumpy state, listening to the Radio One Breakfast Show emanating from the caravan closest to me and the yells of various folk struggling to control overenthusiastic dogs. This was what I hated about campsites. That morning I felt ill-disposed towards my fellow man and resentful that they were camped around me in hordes. I drank my morning tea while Greg James chatted about his favourite cake and someone from a nearby campervan yelled at Tommy, a Yorkshire terrier who was escaping with his owner's toast. I decided that sitting in the tent feeling sorry for myself was achieving nothing and decided to head for the beach, where the sound of the surf might overwhelm the sounds of the campsite.

On my way to the beach, I met an older couple happily ensconced in their Hot Tent –a tent heated by a woodburning stove. I realised at once that this was the solution to my year-round camping problem. I could be warm and secure all year. I realised that my Hot Tent adventure had begun.

Since that fateful meeting, I have been inspired by using a hot tent. It has opened up a new world for me, to such an extent that my canvas home has inspired me to make journeys and visit places I had never previously considered. This nomadic way of life has put me in touch with the landscape and wild places in ways I had never imagined. This book is the first in a series about my life in a hot tent, exploring Scotland. I hope you will join me on this exploration. I want to share my joy for this land, for its wild terrain and unpredictable weather. If this small series inspires you to follow my example, I'll give you a little advice on how to get started.

Roll up your sleeping bag. Lace up your boots. Pack up your tent and stove and let us wander together.

Chapter 1
Lightweight Camping in the Land of the Midge

It's pitch dark and the wind has dropped. I shine my head torch through one of the vents on my tent but can see nothing beyond the nylon walls. Despite that, they are out there. Lying back in my sleeping bag, I can hear something, so faint as to be barely discernible. There is no denying, however, that the sound is there. A constant, unchanging hum fills the air. It reminds me what is waiting outside.

The hum is the beating of a billion wings. Midges; the air outside the tent is thick with them. I have hidden inside my little nylon shelter for the last five hours. The doors are sealed up. Every zip is closed tight so the midges and their ferocious little jaws can't get in. If I couldn't have kept them out of my lightweight two-man tent, then my time here would have been an unbearable, itching misery. But they are outside, and they know something I am also acutely aware of –I can't stay inside my tent forever. They are waiting in their hundreds, probably thousands, for the moment I have to open my tent door. Then they will feast.

Some of you reading this will think I am exaggerating. Perhaps you are thinking that these are only insects and, though irritating, how bad can they be? Then there will be others, those who have experienced the full force of the amassed Highland midge. They will not be thinking I exaggerate. In fact, they will not be thinking at all –they will be scratching. They won't be aware of it but their fingertips will already be seeking out the sites of midge bites of old. As they read this their hands will be making involuntary waving motions, brushing away imaginary midges. They may even have forgotten battles fought against these tiny beasts. Their minds may have forgotten, but their bodies have not and so, without even knowing it, they have begun to scratch.

~

In the summer of 2020 I, along with everyone else in Britain, eventually came out of lockdown after the first wave of the Covid-19 pandemic. I had spent long, isolating days locked inside my flat in Inverness, fearful of the plague that raged outside. The five-mile travel limit imposed by the government kept me away from the hills. Bereft of my favourite outlet in life, I sank into lethargy and found myself staring out of the window in a bewildered torpor. Gradually the restrictions are lifted, and by July I am free to head out into the wilder areas of my Highland home once more.

My plan is to head down to Glen Affric, just over an hour

9

from my home. Glen Affric is a special place, a great V-shaped valley running across the Highlands from east to west. It begins abruptly in a steep-sided gorge near the tiny village of Cannich and then winds its way between hills shrouded in forests until, after long winding miles, the glen widens again. Here, Loch Beinn a' Mheadhoin winds its way further west with steep forests falling into its waters. Further west still, the glen widens to where the hills once again rise in endless sweeping ridges. Here Loch Affric sits, reaching towards the head of this deep, remote glen. I have walked here many times, yet the scale of this landscape always leaves me in awe. This glen in autumn, when the forests blossom with colour as the leaves change to shades of gold and russet browns, is one of the finest sights in all of Scotland. In winter, its ridges offer long undulating walks over lonely ice-covered ridges. In summer, too, it has its charms; its tree-covered hills make this one of the greenest and most verdant of all the glens of Scotland. It is a joy at any time of year.

I want to camp beside Loch Affric. I know the hazards of the biting beasts but I am hoping that if I am close to the shoreline then there will be a breeze to keep them off me. Midges may be ferocious biters but they are weak fliers; any breeze over seven miles per hour will ground their squadrons. After the interminable lockdown, I long to be able to travel anywhere that takes me away from the concrete and tarmac of the city streets. I need to be out in the wild wind again, far from the sound of a car engine. I want to be alone with the hills again.

I am apprehensive as I drive up the glen, following the narrow road as it hugs the hillside. The media has been full of reports of a countryside invasion of campervans, caravaners and wild-campers. People who, like me, have at last been released from lockdown and are desperate to find some green-space camping. There are images of laybys and grass verges buried under mobile homes, with tents invading every open space and wild places defiled by campers using scenic Scotland as a toilet. According to some Scottish newspapers, the whole population of Birmingham has abandoned their semi-detached houses and now lives in a layby a few yards north of the sleepy Highland village of Durness. These hordes are now entertaining themselves by littering our countryside with pop-up curry houses and turning the single-track roads into versions of the Spaghetti Junction. I'm worried in case the Highlands I once knew is gone forever. There are voices clamouring for legislation to end the wonderful access rights that have allowed me to wander the hills unfettered, camping or sleeping in bothies wherever I like, for so many years.

Driving up the glen, I notice a handful of campervans and some green tents pitched down by the loch shore. The mass of campervans that I feared is nowhere to be seen and all the tents seem to be pitched responsibly. I've heard reports that areas have been inundated by hordes of people visiting the Highlands for the first time, mainly people whose foreign holidays have had to be cancelled because of travel restrictions –areas such as Glen Coe, Glen More in the Cairngorms, or sections of the North Coast 500, where a great marketing campaign has increased visitor numbers without any investments in infrastructure to support them.

Encouraging people to travel to a remote part of the country where there simply aren't enough places for them to park or sufficient toilets for them to use, and where the single-track roads are unable to handle the sheer volume of traffic, is bound to lead to problems. Surely we should not blame people who have been under virtual house arrest for months for wanting to escape to one of the most beautiful parts of our country. Perhaps we in the Highlands need to show a little more tolerance, even if the people who come here do inadvertently leave damage in their wake. Our press looks for villains and often finds them in the people who are victims. Has not the Highlands been marketed on shortbread tins and grannies' postcards for decades in pursuit of the tartan pound? If the tourist board has been telling people to come here all this time, we cannot moan when they show up.

I arrive in the forest car park at the end of the road. As I step out of the car the scent from the tall pines greets me. I can hear the waters of the river raging below and the sound of birdsong. These are the scents and sounds of the hills; my heart leaps to know them again after so long. As I haul my rucksack on, the midges begin to find me. At first there are only one or two irritating pin pricks, which I try to ignore. Soon, this increases as my attackers zero in on me. Within moments, I begin performing a sort of avant-garde jazz dance as I try to ward off the hordes of minute vampires. Movement is the only real defence against the midge. They are such poor fliers that it takes them time to locate a stationary target and build up in sufficient force to make life unbearable.

Once out of the shelter of the forest car park, a slight breeze comes across the loch and the midges relent a little. To my left the hills rise verdant with forest, and to my right the loch sits sparkling below me, a great body of water sitting beneath far hills and endless ridges. Walking along the forest road, I cannot believe that I am back in the open hills once more. The long, long days and weeks of lockdown had begun to assume an air of permanence. It was as though the life I had known before had gone. The world outside my flat slipped into memory. I felt like a prisoner who has been locked up for so long he has grown used to the walls of his cell and considers them the only reality. Walking along that forest road, it was as if I had walked out of the prison gates. I half expected someone to blow a whistle and to suddenly hear the voices of my jailors hurrying after me.

I am free at last.

A few miles from the road end, Glen Affric is the way it has always been: huge, spectacular and empty. There are no hordes of folk camping in every available space. In fact, there is no one here at all. It is as it always was; all through the long months of lockdown it has been waiting for me. The midges attack me as I fumble with my tent, out of practice with its poles and zips. It is too early to sit in my tent yet –the sun is still peeping over the hills, and I'll overheat in my tent if I get in now. I do the only thing I can; I go for a walk. After weeks of lockdown, I am overwhelmed by the sheer scale. I have spent months in the confines of my flat or walking through city streets, with occasional supermarket trips. Endless days in a shrunken world, life shrivelled by fear. Now it's hard to adjust to a natural world that has become unfamiliar. How quickly we forget the wide open skies, the scent of heather and water, and the stillness of the hills and lakes. Walking on that hillside, I realise that I am released from my prison but not yet free of its walls.

I walk for a couple of hours along the lochside, lost in a kind of trance, trying to readjust to freedom. Mesmerised by the space and the simple but treasured pleasure of being able to go wherever my boots take me. When at last the summer sun begins to dip behind the hills on the far side of the loch, I return to my tent. The trick now is speed. I have to get into my tent without the hordes of waiting midges joining me inside. I walk away from the tent slowly, followed by a black cloud. Several yards from the tent I turn and sprint for my shelter. The midges are momentarily confused; it takes them a second or two to realise where I've gone. Before they can regroup, I unzip the door of my Vango two-man tent, and leap inside, zipping shut the insect-proof doors behind me. It works. Only a few of the winged demons make it inside.

I spend the night listening to the silence. I have missed this quiet. This other world, far from the sounds of the city. The only thing between me and the stars is a thin sheet of nylon. Having spent several months in the close proximity of others, I have forgotten what it is like to know that the nearest person must be several miles away.

My tent is spacious for one person, although it would be pretty snug for the two people it is designed for. In the morning, I realise there is something else that I have forgotten about camping, which is how to put my trousers on in a confined space. It takes me a while to find them. They seem to have moved around during the night. Eventually I find them hiding under my sleeping mat. I push my foot into one leg and try to pull them up but they won't move. After struggling for several minutes, I realise my foot is in a pocket. I try again, find a leg, and the struggle begins again. After grunting and performing a horizontal limbo dance, I pull the leg up. There's only one problem: it's the wrong leg. It would be easier for a butterfly to get back into its chrysalis. After several minutes of battle, I am eventually trousered. At least the isolation of this spot ensures no one has been able to witness an old man in battle with his nether garments.

Midges may not be very smart, but they are patient. They have waited outside my tent all night. They cluster in great clouds outside the vents of my tent. There is a reason they are there. They are not like other flying creatures, drawn by light. They are attracted to something more sinister: my breath. I can lie in my tent in the dark and stay silent, but that won't keep me safe. They can smell me. So they wait, knowing I'll come out eventually.

They are right: I wake thirsty and desperate for a pee. As soon as I open the tent door, they descend on me in their thousands. After a few moments peeing, the details of which are not fit for publication, I light my stove to boil water for tea. All the while, I am twitching and slapping myself and performing odd gyrations –the dance of a thousand midges. While I am doing this, I begin to take down the tent. There is only one thing to do: escape. I pull on my midge hood, a sort of fine net that covers my head. Without it, the persistent bites would be intolerable. With it, I can just about function. The air around me is a thick soup of tiny, winged insects. I am praying for wind but the surface of the loch below me remains mirror calm, reflecting the green hills above. It must be a perfect scene, but myriad jaws are focussing my mind on survival. I pour a mug of tea, eager for a brew in the early morning. In order to drink I have to raise the midge hood. As I do so, the midges, summoned by some unheard bugle call, stage a mass charge towards my face. As I take my first sip, the tea has an odd texture. The surface of the brown liquid has turned black as several thousand kamikaze midges drown themselves in my morning brew. I am determined that these cursed creatures will not deprive me of my tea and drink it, midges and all. They have been eating me for years, so it's only fair I consume a few of them.

I'm just gulping down my tea-and-midge soup when a woman appears on a shiny red mountain bike. She is gasping for air, sweat dripping from her face. I know why she has been pedalling so hard: she dares not stop, or the clouds of midges will descend on her. She is so surprised to see me she halts for a moment. I guess she is around forty and she peers at me, red-faced, from beneath her midge net. She is breathing heavily and there is no mistaking the look of abject desperation on her face.

The midges have taken their toll. I attempt a cheery wave, hoping to encourage her. There is a strange sensation as my hand moves through the air. It feels as though my fingers are pushing against a fine net curtain. It is midges –the air is so thick with them it has turned semi-solid.

In between gasps of breath the cyclist tries to speak but each time she tries to form a sentence the evil cloud around her forms up for another charge. She begins to gyrate with increasingly frenetic movements, alternating between scratching herself and slapping her exposed calves and forearms. She just doesn't have enough hands. I would probably have found this funny if I had not been doing exactly the same thing myself.

In the end she manages to stammer, "Keep moving." With that, she stands on the pedals of her bike and exits, followed by clouds of voracious jaws. I doubt she'll stop until she cycles into the sea on the far side of Scotland.

I cram my tent and its contents into my rucksack and make a break for it. Once I am moving, the midges become more bearable. After two hundred yards a miracle occurs: a slight breeze starts up. It's not much of a wind but the midges are forced to take refuge in the long grass. With the thick insect soup diminished, I can at last take off my midge hood and breathe again. Even though I was encased in a nylon shell and besieged by teeming midges, I had at least been free of the confines of my flat for the night and slept among the hills while the sun had slipped lazily behind the high ridges of the mountains.

Even though the chances of escaping to a mountain bothy

will still be remote for many months to come, I have been able to recapture something of the joy I feel in spending my nights in the hills. The secret of happiness is simple, or so they say: find out what makes you happy and do it. It has taken me a long time to discover the truth in those words. At night in the hills I feel a peace I experience nowhere else. Sitting in a lonely bothy I may not be as comfortable as I am in my centrally-heated flat. I am bereft of central heating and a widescreen TV. I can't get a cold beer from the kitchen whenever I want one. Yet, out in the hills, I am free.

Every time I throw on my rucksack and walk off into the hills, or even just spend an hour watching the waves breaking on some far northern shore, I have broken free. In those minutes and hours, I have ceased to be a commodity and the great beast, having no use for me, turns away in search of new and more willing victims. As I walk back to my car, under the unfamiliar weight of my pack, it is as if I have escaped from the nightmare of lockdown when I was imprisoned in my own flat, reduced to waiting for the next news bulletin or searching the internet for the latest information on the scourge of Covid-19. The miasma of fear that surrounded me then is slowly beginning to disperse. It will take time for the shroud of that disaster to be lifted. I have to accept that it will take me some time to feel comfortable in the wild again. I won't just snap back to where I was when Boris Johnson announced we were moving into lockdown at the end of March 2020.

The car park I've left my little black Skoda in is

surrounded by trees that shelter it from the faint breeze which I was so grateful for. Here the midges return with renewed ferocity, and I am forced to retreat beneath my mesh hood as I hurl my rucksack into the car and take off my boots. Just as I am about to drive away, a VW campervan, like the one Scooby Doo used to travel in, pulls up beside me.

The occupant, a bespectacled middle-aged man, winds the window down half an inch. "Have you been camping?" he asks incredulously.

"Yes, just down the glen."

He peers at me suspiciously through the tiny gap in the window. "What were the midges like?"

There's no point in lying. "Horrendous."

There's a mechanical hum as he closes the window. I can see it's already too late for him. While he was speaking to me, several thousand tiny black assassins flooded into his car. He is already slapping his face and cursing.

Driving back down the forest road through Glen Affric, my car windows wide open and fan on full to blow my tiny persecutors out of the car, I realise I have a problem. The assault of the midges has reminded me why I long ago abandoned camping in favour of spending my nights in the wild in bothies. No matter how formidable their numbers are, midges will not enter a bothy.

On the way back to Inverness, driving through the rolling countryside of the Moray Firth, I realise that what I need is a mobile bothy. I dismiss the idea of a campervan fairly quickly. Not only can I not afford the exorbitant cost of one of these plastic palaces, I just can't see myself driving around the Highlands in a van with all the modern conveniences of life crammed into a small space. Lots of folk enjoy the freedom that campervans give them and their devotees are as passionate about them as I am about bothies. I have fond memories of sitting in my friend's campervan on holiday in Conwy in Wales. I'm guessing I must have been about eight years old. My dad had decided to take me camping, which was a great idea. The only problem was we didn't own a tent, so he borrowed an army tent from a friend. This, it turned out, wasn't a good idea. The tent was big enough for a battalion and was so heavy he could barely lift it. As my dad didn't drive, we went by train. It took two black cabs to transport us and our equipment to the station in Bebington. We had so much gear we looked more like we were embarking on a polar expedition than heading for a weekend in Wales. My memory is of trying to survive gale-force winds and torrential rain while the tent billowed about, buffeted by the wind. I'm guessing that the weather was a lot kinder than my childhood memories relate. At eight years old, it was a great adventure.

Fortunately for me, a school friend was staying close by in his parents' VW campervan. The family took pity on me and invited me into their little mobile home. I can remember sitting warm and dry in the protection of their van, drinking hot chocolate and watching rivulets of condensation trickle down the window panes. Outside the van, my father struggled manfully to heat a can of chicken soup over a little gas stove. The wind was such that after twenty minutes of effort I was presented with a lukewarm mug of soup. Like all meals eaten in the outdoors, it was one of the most delicious things I'd ever tasted. My friend's van made the adventure bearable, even if the flapping tent kept both my dad and I awake for most of the night. In retrospect, I endured –rather than enjoyed –that camping weekend and it's surprising I ever wanted to go outside again. Childhood memories have a way of glossing over the discomfort, as everyone knows. I'm sure there are many folk who feel affection for the campervans of their youth but I prefer to leave the plastic and Formica surfaces behind. I am a hopeless romantic. I prefer candlelight or a flickering paraffin lamp to electricity.

Having ruled out a campervan, it seems that a tent is my only option. The problem is: which tent? I already have a number of considerations. It has to be big enough for me to stand up in for the purposes of trouser-raising. I have to be able to heat it in some way if I am to enjoy nights in it through the winter, as I would have done in remote bothies. I also want to be able to sit in a chair so that I can avoid the numb shoulders I had experienced in my previous camping exploits. I am certain of one thing: any tent able to fit that bill will not be one that I can roll up and fit into the bottom of my rucksack. It will not be a backpacking tent.

I begin scouring online camping catalogues. Finding a tent that will meet my needs is difficult. The many "family" tents that grin at me from the pages of camping suppliers' catalogues, with multiple doors and huge spacious rooms, look attractive but are too large for what I want. I need a tent that allowed me to stand and move about, but which will also be small enough for me to have some chance of keeping the place warm in winter. In the end, I decide to go for something like the old bell tent design, with a single central pole and a conical shape. This means that I should be able to stand up, and that the interior of the tent will be reasonably compact and therefore possible to heat, perhaps by using paraffin lamps.

None of the tents from mainstream suppliers fit the bill. One afternoon, I find a tent on Amazon that looks as though it could be right. It is the bell shape I am looking for. It is reasonably light for the sort of tent I want, coming in at about seven kilograms. I've never heard of the manufacturer. It is made in China, like pretty much everything else these days, and, at around a hundred pounds, it is very reasonably priced. I click the order button and sat back, awaiting my tent.

Chapter 2
Let There Be Light

The difference between a good idea and catastrophe is a fraction of a second.

On the Scottish west coast peninsula of Morvern, it has been known to rain for weeks and even months. This particular November afternoon, as I walk up the three-mile track to Crosben bothy, it is raining hard enough to raise Noah from his grave and have him getting out the ark plans. Huge drops of water plummet from the heavens and bounce off the hood of my cagoule. As I walk through the wooded ravine, the river roils below me, its waters stained black and malevolent with peat. Just when I think it can pour no harder, another squall, even more vicious than the last, sweeps down from the hills. I'm on my way to meet one of my bothy companions who I have named 'the colonel' because of his addiction to wearing ex-army outdoor gear. He and I have spent many nights in the far-flung corners of Highland glens enjoying the dubious pleasures of icy bothies.

I walk on and try to keep my spirits up. It's times like this I am grateful for the quality of my waterproof gear. Despite the deluge, my Paramo jacket and trousers refuse to let even a drop of water reach my skin. This gives me some consolation; I'm confident I'll make it to the bothy before the rain can get through my waterproofs. I have learnt to accept whatever the Highland weather produces with a Zen-like acceptance.

I've never forgotten when I met an elderly Highland lady in a village beside Loch Ness. It was a day like this and she was clearly getting soaked.

I pulled up beside her in my car. "Can I give you a lift? It's pouring down."

She smiled at me as though she hadn't noticed the rain until I pointed it out. "Och, it'll no get past my skin."

I always think of her when I'm in weather like this; the trick is to ignore it. There's a ruined cottage about half a mile from the bothy. By now, in normal conditions, I would get my first sight of the two-storey cream-coloured building. Today it is hidden by the veil of rain. I pick my way through a flooded bog and then, even more cautiously, across a dilapidated bridge that groans ominously under my weight. The stream beneath is swelled to three times its normal size and I unfasten my rucksack, anxious in case the bridge gives way and hurls me into the waters beneath.

Minutes later, I am standing saturated in the bothy, dripping water forming pools around my boots. It's dark by now and the colonel emerges from the bothy's only warm room. He is dressed as usual in green army fatigues, his brass buttons gleaming in the lamplight.

"Wet, was it?" he asks, puffing gently on his pipe.

Three miles of tramping through torrential rain has dampened my sense of humour. I say something curt in reply.

"It was perfectly dry when I walked in up the track," announces the colonel, as he puts a match to his pipe.

I grunt and think dark thoughts about the colonel crashing through the bridge on the way home.

It only takes a few minutes to shed my waterproof shell and emerge, turtle-like, dry and comfortable. As I sit down next to the tall black cast iron stove and feel its heat, my mood softens. I am grateful that the colonel had carried in some coal and got the stove going. We are sat in a small room with a table and a couple of armchairs, with some bookshelves on one wall. It is the perfect size for a bothy lounge. It can hold six to eight folk comfortably but is small enough that the stove can easily keep it pleasantly warm.

"I've finished it," the colonel announces, indicating an impressive lamp standing on the wooden table.

The colonel and I share a passion for paraffin lamps. Sitting in pride of place is an Aladdin lamp. It was probably made in the 1930s. It has a large shade made of something that looks like plastic but isn't. At its centre it has a tubular wick which is incredibly delicate and crumbles at the slightest touch. The lamp gives out enough light to light the room easily and also produces a reasonable amount of heat.

"Brilliant. You made a good job of that."

"Working perfectly." He grins with pride, unable to resist a tweak at the tiny wheel that adjusts the flame. "I installed the new wick today."

We could have brought in an electric torch, which would have lit the bothy more effectively, but there is nothing like a living flame. Candles are effective, but paraffin lamps are much more effective and give a warm light. The lamp's main drawback is that it is temperamental; it's incredibly sensitive to changes in room temperature. It works fine one minute then seconds later it is belching smoke. It takes skill to handle these beasts, and there's the beauty of them. The Aladdin was one of the last paraffin lamps to reach mass production before electric light became available and relegated such lamps to history.

I hang my wet clothes by the stove and we spend the next couple of hours talking and sharing a dram or several while the rain batters against the bothy windows. The lateness of the hour and the conviviality of the time we spend together will influence events to come. We are engaged (as we often are in these days) in discussing the evils of driven grouse shooting, which is a subject both of us are passionate about and our views are made all the more compelling by the amount of whisky we have drunk. So engrossed are we in conversation that we don't notice the temperature of the room falling. Feeling the chill, I turn and open the stove door, revealing a few smouldering embers and the fire close to going out.

"Damn —sorry, I should have noticed it was going down." As I am sat by the fire, it is my job to keep it fed.

"I'll get a firelighter," the colonel announces.

I know we are running low on firelighters and am anxious to preserve the few we have. Then I have an excellent idea.

"Save the firelighter. Soak a paper towel in paraffin and chuck that on."

I can see he is impressed by my clever solution to the problem. He nods and heads off to the store cupboard. I anticipate that the paraffin will vaporise in the warmth that remains in the stove but might not ignite without help, so I light a long wax taper from one of the candles and wait for the colonel.

"This should do it," he says, returning with a paper towel soaked in paraffin.

I open the door of the old stove and the colonel hurls in the towel. The paraffin steams as it hits the warmth of the embers but does not catch light. I pride myself as the skilled master of any bothy fire through years of experience and have the solution to hand –the lit taper. I lean in towards the stove and reach the paraffin vapours with the taper.

Neither of us is entirely certain what happens next. That there is an explosion is beyond doubt. Afterwards, I can recall a vivid flash and a loud bang. The colonel remembers a gout of flame leaping from the door of the stove and across the bothy. He also tells me that, for a gentleman of my age and generous proportions, the backward leap I took as the stove cannoned into the night was exceptional. He had only previously witnessed similar feats in *Batman* films.

I remember colliding with the wall on the opposite side of the room, then rushing to slam the cast iron door on the stove shut in order to cage the flaming beast. Much to my surprise, the bothy windows are still intact.

"We won't do that again, will we?" says the colonel, checking to see if all his brass buttons are still in place.

"No, I don't think we will." I nod, patting out parts of my clothing that are still smouldering.

We sit in silence for a few minutes, waiting for the smoke to clear, then the colonel looks at me oddly. "Has your new tent arrived from China yet?"

Something in the way he asks makes me wonder if he is trying to decide if it is wise spending time with me in a bothy.

"Not yet." Maybe I should keep my ideas to myself.

Chapter 3
The Road to Damascus –Well, Gairloch Actually

I blame John Wayne.

Wayne, in his sheriff's outfit, walks into the barn of the livery stable to get his horse, blissfully unaware that the outlaw Jonny Ringo is hiding behind the door. The dastardly Ringo springs out from behind the door and catches him with what my old Nan would have called a "fourpenny one", right behind the ear. Wayne goes down but, by superhuman effort, rises and hits Ringo with a punch that would have killed the horse. Ringo flies back across the hay, knocking over a hurricane lamp in the process. (Every barn in every western you'll ever see has a lit hurricane lamp inside, despite the fact it's daylight outside; there must be some law about it.) The lamp breaks and a ribbon of flaming liquid runs across the floor and sets the barn alight.

Ringo goes for his gun …

I'm afraid you'll have to make the rest up for yourself.

That western scene has tarnished the image of paraffin lamps in the public imagination forever. If you knock over a hurricane lamp it won't burn down the barn or bothy. Paraffin is pretty safe stuff and is very reluctant to ignite; it needs a wick, unless it's been pre-heated in a stove of course. You can put a match out in a tumbler of paraffin –although please don't as I couldn't afford the legal bills.

This next section is best read in a shed. If you don't have a shed then imagine you are sitting in one surrounded by tools and mechanical devices and reeking, as all sheds do, of oil, old leather and dreams of spiders. You need to be in a shed because I'm going to be talking about paraffin lamps and that's where most of these lamps live. Actually, I won't be talking about lamps –Norman will. Norman is my shed alter ego. He has a grey beard and moustache, a grey cardigan and grey trousers, and knows a lot more than anyone should about the West Midlands Railway. For God's sake, don't ask him.

Norman smiles and puts down his mug of tea, which has the word "Boss" emblazoned in big letters.

"Now, you see, what you need in that Chinese tent of yours is a couple of paraffin lamps. Keep it nice and cosy, they will. I've used paraffin lamps in bothies –a lot more effective than candles, you know. Mainly I use hurricane lamps."

Norman lifts a lamp down from a shelf. It is like the one Ringo smashed in the barn. It has a wick inside a glass globe, raised by a lever mechanism so that you can light the flame.

"Or you could go for one of these beauties," Norman says, reaching under the table and producing another highly polished lamp. "This is a Tilley, more powerful and very economical on paraffin. I restored this one myself."

Norman proudly displays the pressure lamp. It has a domed base with a tube leading up to an enclosed mantle. It's a much more formidable machine with a cylindrical glass globe and metal top.

"You pressurise it and the paraffin is forced up this metal tube where it's vaporised by the heat." Norman can't resist giving the lamp a couple of quick pumps with the brass primer.

A Tilley works by heating the paraffin in a tube, using a small quantity of methylated spirits, a process known as priming. Primus stoves use exactly the same principle. The vaporised fuel burns inside a sort of wick, known as a mantle. Tilley lamps are pressurised and have a pump that forces the paraffin up the tube to where it burns in the mantle, giving off light and a reasonable amount of heat. Although the mantle is incredibly fragile, it is well protected in a glass cylinder, which is also protected from accidental damage by a number of metal hoops. The advantage of the Tilley over other models of paraffin lamp is that it is robust. Its glass is much less fragile than in other lamps and is protected by metal hoops. Another big advantage is that, once lit, a Tilley gives a very safe, consistent flame and isn't prone to flaring up or smoking, as many other types are. The disadvantage is that they are pretty heavy, coming in at around two kilograms.

Norman is warming to his subject.

"Now, this beauty here," says Norman, taking down from

the shelf a glittering lamp with a tall glass chimney, "is a duplex. Two wicks, see. Burns a bit more paraffin but gives a lovely light."

He produces a box of matches and touches the wick of the lamp. Immediately, the shed is filled by a warm yellow glow, made brighter by the highly polished brass body of the lamp.

Norman's eyes glow with satisfaction. "Polished her up me self. See your face in it now."

He holds up the lamp and a distorted image of his grey beard appears on the bowl.

"Now then," says Norman, admiring his lamp, "did I ever tell you about the West Midlands Railway …"

Quick, run for it!

~

Back from the shed now and, in my defence, I know nothing about the West Midlands Railway. I thought I'd let Norman tell you about paraffin lamps and save me the trouble.

After a quick look on eBay I order a Tilley lamp while waiting for my Chinese tent to arrive. What I didn't realise when I ordered this tent was that not only was it made in China, but it would have to come from China. After three weeks I am wondering if the bloke who made it is personally carrying it all the way. The lamp arrives before the tent and I spend a happy day in my shed with Norman, restoring it to working order. A few days after that, my Chinese tent finally appears.

I pack my car in Inverness for my new adventure. I've got

my Tilley lamp and my camping chair and now, of course, my Chinese tent. I am about to try to establish my first mobile bothy. The spot, next to a ruined cottage by the side of Loch Loyal, seems idyllic even though, as I unpack my car, I can't resist a longing glance across the grey waters to where one of my favourite bothies, Achnanclach, sits.

I have spent many nights alone there, sitting beside the fire and listening to rain being hurled against the roof by the wild Atlantic winds. How much I would have liked to walk the few miles up past the loch and sit before that fireplace today! This, however, is October 2020 and all bothies are closed by the Covid-19 pandemic. So here I am, trying to find a way to replace the little shelters that have been such an important part of my life.

This part of Sutherland is empty even in the tourist season. In October, the campervans and motorbike tourists have long departed. I am so excited to be here again and to have a chance to regain the freedom that means so much to me. I unpack my new tent and unfurl it on the ground. In this instant, my good idea turns into a mistake.

The great danger in buying things off the internet is that the images that you see on screen are often deceiving. What looks large and comfortable on the screen turns out to be small and tight-fitting when you actually hold it in your hands. The tent was the right shape, I had decided, and looked solid in the picture. When I actually unpack it I realise that, although the shape is right, the tent is far too flimsy to withstand the Highland weather.

I erect it in minutes, but as soon as it is up, the wind threatens to tear it down. When I say wind, I am exaggerating. The gusts that are hitting this tent and caving its sides in are not what Sutherlanders would consider wind at all. This is a breeze, or even less than that perhaps; just the mere hint of a breath from the slumbering giant of the Atlantic. I can see that this tent was no match for the Highlands, but I refuse to give in. I set up my little shelter and erect my chair. I spend the evening grabbing onto the centre pole of the tent as the breeze tosses it from one side to the other. I light the Tilley lamp and it hisses away manfully, but there is so much wind passing through the tent that there is no way the lamp can raise the temperature. I spend the evening grabbing onto the centre pole of the tent as the breeze tosses it from one side to the other. I light the Tilley lamp and it hisses away manfully, but there is so much wind passing through the tent that there is no way the lamp can raise the temperature. I spend most of the night clinging to the pole like a cowboy desperately trying to stay in the saddle of a wildly bucking mustang. Feeling defeated and not a little stupid, I sit in my sleeping bag trying to work out what the hell I had been thinking when I bought the tent.

It had seemed such a good idea. It is exactly the shape I've been looking for and is even light enough for me to carry over reasonable distances. The only difficulty, and this is now blindingly obvious, is that there is no way this tent will withstand the rigours of the Highland winters. It is incredibly well ventilated, presumably to help with the humid air of a tropical climate. There is nothing wrong with this tent provided you don't try to pitch it in a Highland glen.

In the morning, I awake to find my belongings scattered about the tent by the wind. Fortunately I am able to sleep through pretty much anything, which is just as well as my tent looks as if a herd of wildebeest have spent the night running through it. With the skies threatening rain and the wind rising, I pack up my damp tent and even damper spirits, head home, post the tent back to China, and spend a few months looking at what tents are available, trying to find another solution.

It's May. At least that's what the calendar says, but me the gales of wind coming in from the sea make it feel like mid-October. The campsite in Gairloch is full of tents so big you could spend several days searching for the exit. They are great hooped monstrosities with windows and awnings, full of pockets and zips and multiple rooms. They are the kinds of plastic palaces I had always vowed I would never own, yet here I am, slowly unfolding one of these monsters and trying to decide which hoop goes in which sleeve and how to handle the vast array of buffeting nylon I am confronted with.

There's just so much tent and most of it seems determined to take off down the campsite and carry me out to sea. The gusts of wind are accompanied by intermittent deluges of rain. I can see one coming; a great grey curtain is sweeping in across the waves. It will be here at any moment and my tent is still lying at my feet. I have managed to get the hoops through all the sleeves but each time I try to erect the tent, the wind grabs the walls and I am launched into a pitched battle with an unseen monster. There is no doubt about it: I am not winning right now, and I can feel eyes on me as I wrestle the acres of nylon fabric in the rising wind. All around me, caravaners and mobile-home dwellers are watching my struggle, no doubt commenting to each other, between mouthfuls of digestive biscuits and sweet tea, about how glad they are not to be in some awful tent. The last thing I want is some kind person to come over and offer to help. If I can't put the thing up on my own, then this purchase too is a failure.

I get the three hoops in and my tent starts to take shape – I'm winning at last! It's at this point that one of the zipped doors flies open and the accumulated rain from the roof pours in, forming a pool two inches deep in the porch. One of the hoops has jammed in the fabric and I give it a mighty shove to get it into place. There's a crack as a split appears about eight inches long down the length of a section of pole. I can't decide if the thing was faulty at the start, or whether my overenthusiastic shoving was to blame. Either way, now is not the time to worry. Despite being damaged, the pole holds and I am at last able to haul the tent into shape and get the poles in. The tent is up!

It's at this point that the rain stops. I like to think that I am able to erect pretty much any tent single-handedly, although I am forced to concede that getting this fairly average five-birth tent up in even moderately windy conditions has been challenging to say the least. To have had someone come over from their warm van and offer a helping hand would have been bad enough but if I'd had to actually ask for help, my credentials as an old hand at this outdoors stuff would have been damaged forever.

Once inside the tent I am sheltered from the elements, but even this heavyweight family tent is at the mercy of the winds and buckles with the impact of each rising gust. I set my seat up and wrestle with the kitchen. The kitchen is a set of folding wire shelves with a wind shield and a flat metal work surface on the top so you can cook. It has been designed by a geometry fiend. Only if you fold it in exactly the right order is it possible to erect it. It has three shelves. I fold two perfectly and get them to engage in the little slots that hold them in place. Then I realise that one shelf is not locked. I have to unlock the other two to get that locked in place and then, of course, one of the first two refuses to lock. Whoever constructed this thing was sacked from IKEA for being too evil to design flat-packed furniture. Finally, after a lot of swearing, some forcing, and a bit of surreptitious bending, I manage to get the shelves erected and fairly stable.

I find the folding kitchen great for storing things in once it's erected, and it also has the massive advantage that I don't have to cook on the floor. I feel almost civilised. My next step is to light my Tilley lamp. I fill the little pincer-like priming pan with meths, give the cylinder a few pumps to get the pressure up, and light the methylated sprits. I really enjoy watching the blue flame dance around the fuel pipe of the lamp. I'm really fond of old technology.

The Tilley lamp emits a gentle glow, so different from electric light which is clinical, harsh and brings with it the modern era. Holidays should be an escape from the mundane, the everyday. You should feel as though you have been transported somewhere different. The blue flame dies and I turn the little knurled knob that will release the paraffin up into the burner. No matter how many times I light a Tilley lamp, this is always a tense moment. If I haven't used enough meths the fuel will flare in the burner and I will have to close the valve, wait for the lamp to cool down and start the process all over again.

This time there's a loud pop as the vapour hits the heated mantle. There are three more such flashes −these are air pockets in the fuel pipe pushing their way out. The flame dies and paraffin vapour hisses out. I have to be quick now. If I am too slow, the vapour will cool in the fuel pipe and condense, leaving soot and flames flickering above the lamp. I strike a match and apply it close to the mantle. There is another pop and the lamp lights. It gutters for a moment and then stabilises, filling the tent with a warm, gentle glow. Now the lamp is lit, it will stay that way for hours. I've no need to touch it again. I sit back in my chair, pour a whisky and listen to the gentle hiss of the lamp.

These lamps have history. They lit the trenches of the First World War. The polar explorers Shackleton and Scott basked in the glow of such lamps and would have found comfort, just as I do, in the gentle purring of the lamp. I'm not a polar explorer and I'm actually sat in a nylon family tent on a warm evening –but a man can dream.

I am warm enough in the tent on this mild night, but the struggle I had getting it erected alone and the battering from the wind it has taken have convinced me that there is no way this tent would be able to survive a Highland storm. I am going to have to find something much stronger.

The following morning, I take a stroll along the beach and the magic of the west coast of Scotland greets me. Cloud has drifted in overnight and now shrouds the hills, bringing their ridges and glens into sharp contrast. A few miles away across the sea, the hills of the rugged Trotternish peninsula of the Isle of Skye stand green in the morning sun. The mountains are steep and rocky and, by contrast, the clouds that cover them are duvet soft. It is the light that strikes me most, as well as the immense space that I have learned to treasure again after the restrictions of the pandemic. I immerse myself in a scene that carries my gaze across the deep green of the sea and loses my imagination in the mist-shrouded hills. For a few minutes, walking along the beach with my boots crunching in the sand, I am lost in a view that has been immutable for a thousand years. In all that time, children have been born, lived, loved, and have themselves returned to the sand, yet this view has barely changed. The sea has washed against this beach, just as it does now, since the beginning of time. I can do nothing but stare in wonder. I take a few photographs, knowing that the camera has no chance of catching anything more than a poor two-dimensional shadow of this infinite place. I spend an hour or so on the beach just looking at the sky and the sea and letting the sound of the waves slow my breathing and my thoughts. At last, I turn back to make myself breakfast in my newly acquired plastic palace.

As I walk along the narrow sandy path back through the dunes to the campsite, I catch sight of an odd-looking tent. It is canvas, not nylon like all the others on the site, and, strangest of all, it has a chimney poking out of the roof. When I was a child my father used to read *The Wind in the Willows* to me. There is a story in the book in which Toad, always flitting from one adventure to another, sees a motor car for the first time and is instantly enraptured. For me, this is my moment. I realise instantly that this is the kind of tent I had been looking for. If any tent can withstand the rigours of a Highland winter, then this has to be it.

I have heard that such tents existed but had been doubtful. Tents and fire just don't mix. Since my earliest camping trip with my friend Martin, when we set out to cover the 270 miles of the Pennine Way equipped with a "tent" that was actually a bed sheet stretched over two poles, I must have seen half a dozen tent-versus-fire showdowns. The result has been the same in each and every one of them. Fire: one–tent: nil. All that ever remains of the tent is a smouldering rectangle and, if you're lucky, the disconsolate tent occupant looking down at the charred remains of his pride and joy. Yet here is a tent with a chimney. It just doesn't make sense.

I begin to examine the tent carefully. It is a bell tent, a conical shape supported by one central pole. It is a similar design to my ill-fated Chinese tent, except that this tent has been constructed to withstand the rigours of winter weather and the oriental tent was not. The tent is anchored to the floor by strong nylon straps fitted with tensioners, and each of the ground anchors is backed up by guys running up to the apex of the tent. On the pinnacle of the tent there appears to be a sort of conical canvas hat that has a vent open in it. This tent is unlike any I have seen over the last forty years, but it does look as if it is just what I am looking for.

I am wandering around the tent, taking note of its features, when a small hobbit-like man emerges from inside. He looks a few years older than me, perhaps in his early seventies. He sports a white beard and a Nordic-style woollen hat and doesn't seem the least bit surprised to find me peering at his dwelling.

I decide to take the initiative. "Hello, can I ask you about your tent?"

I have noticed that the tent, although in pretty good order, is far from new. By far the best people to ask about any piece of gear are the folk who have used it year in, year out. People trying to sell you a product will often claim anything about it. I've often found that folk in outdoor shops have far less experience than me and appear to have gone on training courses where they are instructed to say the first thing that comes into their head rather than actually admit they don't have an answer.

The hobbit-like gentleman –whose name, it transpires, is Gary –is more than happy to talk about the tent. I realise that this canvas creature is such a rarity in the Scottish hills that he is used to being asked questions about it by intrigued strangers; I suspect he rather enjoys it.

"How long have you had it?" I ask, trying to find out just how much experience this man actually has.

"Oh, must have had this hot tent over five years now," he beams. "We must have spent over five hundred nights in it."

So this is a hot tent. I've heard the phrase before but never seen one in the flesh. It's obvious that I've found someone who not only can tell me all I need to know about these tents but is also more than willing to do so. All over Britain there are men and women with hobbies, people who are passionate about everything from canal barges to egg cups or growing the largest marrow in the county. It's one of the things we excel at in the UK. Only the USA can boast folk even more fanatical about their pursuits than the British. Sadly, in the USA the obsession with firearms means that a fanatical outdoorsman is likely to be armed to the teeth as well as passionate about a particular type of shelter. Fortunately, here in the UK I can be confident that this woolly-hatted tent obsessive is very unlikely to have an AK47 underneath the tent flap.

He swells with pride. "We've been north of the Arctic Circle in this."

Now he really has my interest. If you can travel that far north with one of these tents, then it should be able to cope with everything a winter Sutherland glen could throw at it.

He gives me the guided tour and points proudly to the tent's storm guys. "I've got everything backed up."

I pride myself in my ability to erect a tent but this man's construction is a work of art. Each guy line comes out at exactly the right angle and everything is under perfect tension. Every peg is inserted just right and has another peg attached behind it whose sole job is to prevent the first peg from moving. His pegs have pegs!

I've never seen anyone take so much care in setting up a tent. "That's not going anywhere, is it?"

He looks at me with a pained expression. "We had a peg come out last night."

I can see that for him this is an insult from the gods. "Ah, well, the rest held." I launch into a series of questions. "What is the tent like in the wind?"

He grins as if relishing the question. "Never bothers it. I've woken up a few times to find every other tent in the campsite flattened and this still standing."

I nod sagely. "I've heard this is a good shape for shedding wind." It's the same shape as my ill-fated Chinese tent, but I don't mention that.

"The only time I've had any trouble was when we got hit by a katabatic wind on the Isle of Skye." Gary's eyes sparkle as he welcomes the chance to tell me his stories. "Flattened every tent in the glen, including this one. Broke the central pole."

That sounds alarming. "What did you do?"

He smiles contentedly like a man who knows he is equal to any crisis. "I had a spare pole. Had the tent back up in five minutes. No harm done."

Well, of course he had a spare pole; he's a perfectionist. I've experienced a katabatic wind in the Scottish Highlands only once and that was on a winter's day on Ben Nevis's north face, so I know that these are rare and catastrophic events. Katabatic winds are caused when high air, such as that which might sit on the summit plateau of Ben Nevis, cools and becomes denser that the air below. Then, effectively, the cold air mass falls off the high plateau; sometimes they are called fall winds. Frequently, the downdraught is not very fast flowing but sometimes, when the descent is steep –as it is on the north face of Ben Nevis –they can reach hurricane speeds. That is what must have happened to Gary on Skye, and from my experience of these winds I can well understand how no temporary structure, even the strongest tent, could withstand them. He goes on to tell me that there is no rain on Earth that can penetrate the fabric.

"Come and look inside," a voice calls from within.

Gary's wife has been sitting in the tent all this time. It appears she is used to random folk being fascinated by their unusual tent and asking endless questions. Covid-19 restrictions are still in force and I am prohibited from entering any dwelling, so all I do is poke my head inside cautiously. The interior is, of course, as well assembled as the exterior. Gary's wife, a white-haired lady in her sixties, is lounging contentedly at the back of the tent on a low wicker chair. The floor of the tent is covered in sheepskin rugs and there is a sense of luxury inside the canvas shelter.

Gary's wife notices me looking at the deep layers of warm

wool. "You have to insulate yourself from the ground," she explains.

The stove sits horizontally in the heart of the tent. It is a cylindrical object, about the size of a large kitchen bin, supported by curved metal legs hinged onto the body. It is a curious contraption, but most curious of all is the chimney that rises in the form of a steel pipe at one end of the stove and exits through the top of the tent.

This tent is quite unlike any tent I have ever seen before. Gary assures me that the stove is capable of keeping the tent comfortably warm even on the coldest of days.

When I express surprise at this, Gary's wife elucidates. "When it's very cold, the warm air cools a little on the sides of the tent and sinks behind you. It keeps your back warm."

Gary can see that I am impressed with the tent and he gives me a little smile. "Of course, these tents are not for everyone. You have to be a little quirky to own one of these."

I shoot him a quick grin. "That suits me. I am more than a bit quirky."

That night I sit in my nylon family tent, warm and comfortable on a summer's night, knowing that I have seen the ultimate tent. I am a little like Toad who, having seen his first motor vehicle, can think of little else. A quick check on the internet takes me back a little. Tentipi do not produce cheap tents; in fact, Gary and his wife's set-up must have cost over three thousand pounds. For me to get the type of basic set-up that I need, I'd have to pay around two and a half thousand. That's for the Safir 7 tent, a floor and a stove. I've never spent anything like that for any tent. It's much more than I expected, but I begin to weigh up the options overnight. All around me that night on the campsite at Gairloch there are folk sitting in campervans that make the cost of this tent seem incidental. I couldn't buy the bathroom in one of those vans for the cost of this tent, and it's clear that the tent has become a way of life for Gary and his wife.

Chapter 4
Return to Gairloch

For the next few months the countryside is effectively closed. We have become a nation that fears strangers. Covid-19 has made the small communities across the Highlands suspicious of everyone and tourists are not welcome. The fear is that once people are allowed to travel, hordes will descend on the tiny villages of the Highlands and bring the plague with them. It doesn't take long for people to fear those they don't know.

This gives me time to ponder the purchase of my mobile bothy. So, with the luxury of time, I procrastinate. The hot tent is a lot of money. So far, I've spent a few hundred pounds buying the wrong tents. What if I invest my savings in a tipi and don't like it? I would be left with a huge white elephant and a hole in my bank balance. So I do something I'm very good at: look on the internet and ponder.

The nearest stockist for the tent is Nordic Outdoor in Edinburgh, who send me some brochures to look at. I browse those for a few weeks and procrastinate some more. Then I do what I always do when I'm not sure what to do: I ask my daughter, Cat, who lives in Edinburgh and is the most sensible person in the world, what she thinks.

"Why don't you just do it, Dad? You aren't going to suddenly go off the idea of visiting wild places, are you?" she asks in the patient voice she uses when she's pointing out the blindingly obvious to me.

That is it; the decision has been made. Once I decide to do something, I'm always impatient to get it done. In November 2020, as soon as travel restrictions permit, I set off for Edinburgh. I am only allowed to do this because I am able to visit Cat as we are in a "bubble", if you remember those. Looking back now, it seems like another world.

Nordic Outdoor has a number of town centre outlets in the Scottish capital but its HQ and main storehouse is on Granton Road, near the Forth Yacht marina in Edinburgh. They are based in a large green corrugated iron shed that, from the outside, looks like it is about to collapse. Inside, it looks a lot more secure and they have a Safir 7 permanently erected. I decide I will procrastinate no more and sacrifice my credit card. Twenty minutes later, I am heading north up the A9 with my new tent and stove.

A couple of weeks later, with restrictions easing further, I decide to return to Gairloch to see if my new tent can withstand the Highland winter. The forecast is for wind, cold temperatures, snow and hail. There's nothing like jumping in at the deep end, is there?

When I push open the door of the campsite shop, two pairs of eyes regard me suspiciously from the other side of the plastic screen. One pair belongs to a middle-aged woman whose task it is to log people in and out from the campsite. The other pair of eyes belongs to a large black cat who sits on the counter beside the woman. The cat decides that as I haven't come to murder anyone and don't have any fish I can be ignored, and dozes off. The shop is typical of any campsite shop on the west coast. It is crammed with anything the camper could need. Gas cylinders sit on the floor beside rows of tinned beans and a few copies of the local paper.

"Name?" the site owner demands, the list of campsite bookings before her, pen poised, dispensing with the usual niceties of asking about my trip and the weather. She'll shortly know exactly where I've come from, and the weather on this December day is obviously deteriorating rapidly so there is no need to ask.

"Burns," I mutter from beneath my mask.

She grins. "Oh, the nutter in the tent."

It's hard for anyone planning to camp in a tent in December in the Highlands to argue with that label. She was probably right, and I was about to regret spending more than two thousand quid on a bit of canvas and pole. I'm not sure I am a nutter, although I will admit to being slightly eccentric. I have been known to wear a gold-tasselled smoking hat on occasions. I sometimes recite poetry or perform occult rituals as Aleister Crowley at the Edinburgh Fringe, but who doesn't?

I attempt to mount a defence. "It is a very large tent."

I try to sound cheerful. The truth is that this will be my first night in my hot tent and I'm more than a little apprehensive. It's going to be cold tonight, probably windy tomorrow, and there's going to be hail and rain, possibly one following the other, perhaps all at once. I've just spent a lot of money on my tent and, if it can't stand up to these conditions, I've wasted all of it.

The campsite owner ticks off my name in the book; presumably she has the word "nutter" underlined in blue biro beside it. "You can camp beside the toilet block if you like."

Glancing out of the window, I can see the toilet block perched on a hill a few hundred yards away. The wind is picking up already and whipping across the grass behind the toilet block at an alarming speed.

Camping behind a toilet block is not exactly the romantic view I had been hoping for. "I think I might need to find some shelter."

The campsite owner peers at me through the Perspex screen and I can tell by the look in her eyes that she doesn't expect me to survive the night. "Camp anywhere you like."

This is the same campsite I stayed on in July, but it is very different in December. In July, the place was full of children in swimsuits pursued by fathers carrying surfboards, and folk sitting outside their tents beside tables overflowing with tins of beer and packets of snacks. The air was filled with the scent of barbeques and the sound of chattering children. Some of the static caravans do still appear occupied and there are a few of the hardier campervan owners taking shelter in their fibreglass dwellings.

The campsite slopes down to the sea. Higher on the slope

are grassy areas which give way to sand dunes lower down. Beyond the dunes a narrow beach is washed by the white-horsed sea. Looking out over the grey waters I can see a warning of what is coming. Great walls of dark malevolent cloud are barrelling in from the open water as the wind picks up. I have about one hour before the storm makes landfall. I'm not sure that gives me enough time to get the tent secured.

There is a small bowl-shaped area tucked in behind the dunes; I'll get some shelter from the wind there. If I had been sensible, I would have had a dry run in the local park at putting this tent up. Instead, I'll have a very wet run at erecting it with a storm nipping at my heels. Fortunately, for once I read the instructions. It's unlike any tent I have ever erected before. I have to begin by finding the centre spot for my tent, then I place on the ground a plate that indicates the radial angle of the eight pegs that will hold the flysheet of the tent. I have a tape, fixed by a tent peg in the centre of the plate, which gives me the distance that the pegs need to be from the centre. If I get the angle and the distance right, I'll have a ring of pegs that correspond to the main guy lines of the tent.

As I am hammering in the first of the pegs, the wind increases and a few flakes of snow come whipping in from over the sea. All this feels very alien. I must have put up hundreds of tents in all kinds of conditions, but never like this. Any tent I have ever put up has followed the same process. You peg the base out first and then put the poles in; never peg first without any tent. It feels wrong. I reassure myself that I have brought with me my little Vango two-man tent as a sort of lifeboat, in case this canvas monster proves to be a dismal failure. At least I know how to erect the small tent and that it will keep the elements off me if all else fails.

I haul the canvas fly over to the pegs and begin to fix it in position. I get the order of the pegs wrong and have to start again. More haste, less speed. Once all the pegs are attached to the correct rings on the fly, I slot the aluminium pole together and charge into the tent like a medieval spear-carrying warrior. This is the moment of truth. The apex of this bell-shaped tent has a nylon cup, into which the tent pole slots. The only problem is that the cables of the ventilation system also run across this point, and I am confused as to how it all fits together. I push the pole into the centre locater and lift the tent up. Now all the cables are tangled and I have to start again. The centre of the tent has conical-shaped canvas vent covers and I am uncertain as to how these are supposed to fit. On my second attempt, the pole goes in without any tangles and the vent covers slide comfortably into place. As soon the pole is up, the mass of struggling canvas I have been battling with miraculously turns into a tent. I rush round the tent tightening the guys, anxiously looking out to sea where the dark walls of cloud are advancing on me.

The next struggle is to get the floor in place. The tent floor has toggles which locate the eight corners of the tent at each guy line point. The floor has a number of zips that radiate out from the centre. I'm not totally sure what the zips do. Everything feels new and unfamiliar and I'm having trouble working out what goes where. It's like battling with a huge origami puzzle that can fight back in the wind. The floor has to fit under the central pole of the tent, but I can't figure out how. In the end, I have to slacken the guys off for a few minutes, leaving the tent tottering in the wind, and slide the floor under the pole before anchoring the tent again.

"Why the hell didn't you put this thing up in the park first?" I curse.

This is not the time to be finding out how everything works as the Atlantic Ocean is about to empty its contents on top of me. At last, I subdue the floor and tuck the side skirt under it just like that woman said in the instruction video I watched. The only problem is that she was in a field in Kent on a sunny day and I'm on the western coast of the Highlands and I have pissed off the weather god. I tuck the sides of the tent under the floor and the wind instantly blasts the side of the tent out.

A friend has given me an old red carpet that weighs more than the tent and the stove combined. Once I fit the carpet, the tent suddenly takes on an air of luxury. Now for the main event –to unpack the stove. As I haul the box out of the car, the weather turns up in force and pours hailstones down the back of my neck, while the wind grabs the tent and tries to hurl it to the floor. To my surprise, the stove is up on its feet in moments. The chimney is a little more challenging. It's a sort of Russian doll contraption, each section fitting neatly into the other. I get the main chimney together quickly but the mesh tube that disperses the heat confuses me. By this stage, the hail has taken a toll on my hands and my fingers are numb. Eventually, I work out how to fix the little chain that holds the thing together and I can assemble the stove in the tent and finally fix the chimney in place. I still can't get used to the fact that it is possible to have a wood-burning stove in a tent.

It's almost dark by the time I get the rest of my equipment into the tent and fix the storm guys in place. The tent feels a lot more solid now and the elements, for the most part, are kept outside. I've had to weigh down the tent's skirt to prevent the wind from making its way underneath and lifting up the floor, but the tent now feels remarkably secure and the smell of new canvas takes me back to my first experience of camping in the old army tent my father borrowed. At last, I can settle back in my chair and light the old Tilley lamp I bought off eBay. The lamp pops when I try and start it, the result of air getting into the fuel pipe during transit. Seconds later it bursts into life and fills the tent with a warm glow and the gentle hiss of the burner. The tent is transformed instantly. Even though it is still cold, I feel secure in my canvas cocoon and can enjoy the sound of the hailstones being hurled against the tent in the wind.

Next is the step that fills me with most trepidation: lighting the stove. I have lit a great many fires in my time, so getting the thing alight does not worry me. It's what happens next that concerns me. I sit, wondering if I have fitted the chimney correctly. If I haven't got it right, will the tent ignite on my first attempt, leaving me very much the poorer and standing looking at a circle of smouldering canvas?

The campsite owner will be looking from her window, watching the flames leaping into the sky. *I knew he was a lunatic.*

I remind myself that thousands of people must have used a tent like this on countless nights, so the chimney must be insulated enough to protect the tent. With a leap of faith, I put a match to the kindling, close the metal door and hope. Once that wood is alight, there is no way back.

The stove crackles hungrily. From inside, I can hear a low roar as kindling and wood ignite. The stove has come alive, and it creaks and groans as the metal expands. I watch the chimney and the canvas aperture anxiously but, to my relief, there is no sign of anything burning. After two or three minutes, the stove is well alight and I can feel its heat radiating into the tent. I reason that if the tent was going to burn down, it would be alight by now. I can relax. I decide to put my duvet jacket on while I wait for the tent to get warm. When I stand up to reach my jacket, I realise that the tent is already warm. I'm used to bothies that take two or three hours to get comfortable. This tent is different; it has the major advantage of warming up pretty much instantly. This also means that I can heat the tent in the morning if I need to, which is something I've never done in a bothy. It's impossible to carry enough fuel for a fire in the morning and bothies take so long to heat up that the fire would be a waste of time.

Slowly, as the night deepens across the campsite, the wind eases and the hailstorms cease. After my meal, I sit dozing beside the fire. It's so warm that I am down to my tee shirt. In fact, it is almost too warm. Rising above me are cords that open the vents in the top of the tent. The problem is I have no idea how these vents operate, and I worry that if I pull the wrong cord then I might open a vent and not know how to close it. This threatens to expose me to a long, cold night. I decide I am safer to leave this complex system alone for tonight. I'll investigate it tomorrow in the light of day.

The stove has been burning for two hours. If the tent was going to burn down, it would have done so by now. I can relax, confident in the knowledge that I'm unlikely to reduce my little shelter to ash in the near future. I finish reading my book and head out to my car to get another one. Unzipping the tent, I am greeted by a revelation. The wind has died completely and the great clouds that bore down on me so ominously while I was struggling to erect the tent have vanished, leaving a starlit sky glittering over an untroubled sea. Looking up, I see a dreamy vision of starlight and smoke.

Even more surprising than that, the rolling dunes of the campsite have been transformed. The grassy banks glitter with frost crystals in the beam of my head torch and my car is wreathed in ice. Sat in the confines of my tent, beside the wood-burning stove, I had been blissfully unaware of the plummeting temperatures. All that has separated me from this frozen world has been a thin canvas. This is proof positive that the tent can withstand sub-zero temperatures, hail and howling winds.

I have found my mobile bothy.

There is more to this tent than its ability to withstand wind and rain or the extremes of the Highland winter. This tent has something else. It is a modern version of a very old design. The canvas has something no nylon tent could ever have: it has atmosphere. It feels as though Amundsen or Scott could walk in through the door at any moment, kick the snow off their boots, light up their pipes and feel quite at home. They would have been familiar with the gentle purring of the Tilley lamp and aroma of burning wood from the stove. This is a technology that has been used for generations. It is how this tent *feels* that is important. The texture of the heavy canvas and the smell of woodsmoke mingled with paraffin combine to give the sense of moving away from the technology that brought us ultra-light nylon tents and hydrostatic heads. This tent has taken me to a different world.

It is perhaps for this reason I can't see myself in a campervan. The philosophy of the mobile home is very different. The fibreglass and plastic vehicles that roam the Highlands aim to take the comforts we enjoy in our daily lives and allow us to take them with us on our journeys to new places.

This tent is different. It's true that I got wet while I was putting it up. I was cold, lying on the icy ground while I struggled to attach the floor to its toggles. I swore quite a bit when the tent didn't cooperate and when gusts of wind tore the tent from my fingers. Tomorrow, when I get out of my sleeping bag, I will shiver in the frigid air when the stove is cold. The small number of folk who have travelled this far north in their campervans will watch me from behind the plexiglass and wonder why anyone would choose to spend a night in a tent here in the middle of winter. They will be warm and comfortable, and they can take a shower or use their on-board toilet without having to trek across the campsite in the teeth of a gale. There is a crucial difference here, though –they are insulated from the natural world around them while I am immersed in it.

We all need to find a way to experience wild and spectacular places that suits us and our lifestyle. For some it will be the ultra-light wild-camper's tarp stretched over his walking poles, and for others it will be a campervan crammed with the latest tech and costing tens of thousands of pounds. Each has their value and can bring their own special enjoyment. The campervan owner can sit in comfort watching the sun go down over the islands of the west coast. The ultra-light backpacker wakes on a remote mountainside to enjoy a sunrise that he alone will see. Perhaps for me, this canvas tipi will take me to a place where I can live my own dreams. I understand why Gary and his wife so enjoyed meticulously pitching their tent. Over hundreds of nights, they must have perfected their skills in creating the perfect pitch in any conditions. It was something they enjoyed doing, a craft. It is something they can take pride in and perhaps something that we have lost as the convenience of modern life takes us further and further away from the natural world.

We have forgotten that simplicity has a beauty of its own. There can be no more simple structure than a canvas tent stretched over a single pole. If only the rest of our lives could be like that. We have been programmed to crave the new; modern is a watchword we all follow. Yet I feel at ease in this slower world. Perhaps that is why I always felt comfortable beside the fire of a simple bothy in a room lit by candlelight. I had needed to find a place to step off the treadmill and this tent, with the wind sighing in its guy lines, has taken me to that place.

Chapter 5
The Stove

Martin and I have known each other since primary school and we began walking together when we were teenagers. Together, we completed an early trek up the Pennine Way. A few years ago we returned to the route and completed as much of it as we were able to in a nostalgic, if futile, attempt to regain our youth. Martin lives in Blackpool and visits the Highlands two or three times a year, or at least he did before Covid-19 arrived and stopped most travel.

We keep in touch and regularly chat on the phone. Martin is a traditionalist and uses the same design of tent that he used forty years ago.

I call him, full of enthusiasm for my new tepee. "I've got a hot tent. It's great."

"Why is it hot?" he asks slowly, as the cogs of his mind turn.

"It's got a wood-burning stove," I explain.

"A stove? In a tent?" His voice is filled with doubt.

"That's right."

There is a long pause at the Blackpool end of the phone while he considers my last statement. "Doesn't it fill with smoke?"

"No, there's a chimney."

"A chimney?" I can tell he thinks I've gone mad. "And where does the chimney go?"

"Out through the top of the tent," I explain slowly, trying to sound as rational as I can.

"But that'll burn the tent down, won't it?" he asks, adopting the tone of voice you would use to explain to a small child that if he jumps off the roof with cardboard wings he won't be able to fly to America.

"No, there's a cylindrical mesh arrangement that dissipates the heat so the tent can't catch fire."

"Good God!" Martin is almost convinced but has had the same experiences as I have had with tents and fire, and I know he won't be completely sold on the idea until he's seen the tent in action.

"You can keep warm all year round. It's like a mobile bothy."

"This I'll have to see," Martin announces.

When he'll be able to see the tent is anyone's guess.

Martin's reaction is typical of many people when I try to explain how the hot tent works, so it is perhaps worth me saying a little more about the stove at the centre of this tent.

A hot tent without a stove is just a tent. The whole concept of having a stove in a tent was something I struggled to comprehend until my first night in my Safir 7. It was only when I lit the stove on that cold night in Gairloch that I realised what a game-changer a stove really is. I like to think of myself as an expert when it comes to lighting a bothy fire. It can take no small amount of skill to coax a fire out of a bothy hearth that has lain cold and damp for several weeks. I have blown on fires, soaked them in meths, poured paraffin over them; I've burnt sugar and improvised part of a cast iron bed as a tube to blow into the base of a reluctant fire –really important to remember to blow and not suck when you are doing this. Good tip, that one. I have prayed, despaired and sworn at fires pleading with them to light. In my early days I spent a few long nights staring at inert, cold coal I had sweated to carry in to the bothy but which had stubbornly refused to ignite.

When it comes to wood-burning stoves in tents, however, I am a bit of a novice. I'm still learning the art of heating a tent with a stove; like most things in the outdoors, it takes a little practice. The only stove I've used is the Eldfell I bought with the tent. I have some reservations about the Eldfell, which I'll talk about later. If you are reading this book because you are planning to buy a hot tent then I would suggest you ask around for recommendations from people who regularly use hot tents before making your choice. Other models are available and might suit your particular needs or pocket better.

Not only will the stove keep you warm, it will also allow you to dry your clothes and sit comfortably through the coldest night. A hot tent works because no matter how cold and stormy the weather is outside, the stove can produce so much heat you will be warm and comfortable inside. When I first lit my stove, on that icy night in Gairloch, I was staggered by how much heat it produced and how quickly it warmed the tent. As a bothy veteran, I am used to waiting one or two hours before the bothy warms to a comfortable temperature; a hot tent is warm in minutes.

I have found that the problem with the Eldfell stove is that it is a heat demon. The Tentipi tents are designed in Norway, where temperatures below minus twenty are common in winter. In the UK, it's rarely like that. Even in mid-winter, our temperatures mainly hover around freezing point. The coldest night in which I've used my tent in Scotland was around minus ten degrees, which the stove coped with easily. Most of the time, I am trying to keep the stove burning as slowly as possible while it tries to roar away. If you give the stove its head you'll soon be sitting in your underwear looking at a glowing red-hot piece of steel.

The Eldfell stove is a stainless steel drum, about the size of a kitchen bin. It has a door in one end for access to the burning chamber, and a chimney coming out of the top which exits through the top of the tent. The whole thing weighs about twenty kilograms, so backpacking with it over the hills is not an option, although it is still possible to get to some remote locations via a method which I'll talk about later in the book. The tent is protected from the heat of the stove by a large mesh tube that fits around the chimney and can be packed away inside the chamber of the stove, as the sections fit inside each other like a Russian doll. It's a wood-burner so it burns wood –the clue's in the name. I wouldn't burn coal or any other fossil fuel in the stove as I think it would burn too hot and could damage the stove.

It's important to choose the right kind of wood. I only use two types of fuel. By far the hottest is kiln-dried hardwood. This is widely available in most hardware-type shops, although it can be a little harder to find in the summer, when some stores cease selling it, than in the winter. It is also possible to buy unseasoned softwood. Sometimes garages don't know what they are selling, so it is useful to know that unseasoned wood usually comes in netting sacks whereas seasoned usually comes in bags. I never use unseasoned wood as it's as much use as trying to burn ice cream. If it's very cold, I'll go for the hardwood every time. The other type of fuel I often buy, and use more than hardwood, is the kind of compacted logs that are also available. These are frequently made from recycled material and are more environmentally friendly than burning wood. These compacted logs are also designed to burn more slowly than hardwood and so are good if you are looking for a slow release of heat, which I find is best. A wide variety of recycled logs are now available, including coffee logs which have a wonderful aroma; it's best to experiment and find which works best for you. There are some modifications you can make to the stove which will help to control the burn rate. I'll outline these in book three, *Secret Places*.

Although the tent is pretty well ventilated, I always set up a battery-operated carbon monoxide monitor as a precaution. This is especially useful when I am using a paraffin lamp as well as the stove. It's worth remembering that paraffin lamps, and any kind of gas stove, will vent carbon monoxide into the living space of the tent, so care should be taken. Fatalities have occurred where people have sealed themselves inside small tents and used gas stoves for heating.

It is also worth mentioning that charcoal barbeques give off a considerable amount of carbon monoxide, even when they are smouldering and almost out, so they can be very dangerous if you are tempted to bring them into a tent. In all the nights I've stayed in my tent I have never had the carbon monoxide alarm go off, but it is reassuring to have it there. Carbon monoxide can be very dangerous, so a small alarm is a good investment and an important safety feature. It is possible to have an open fire in a tepee by removing the ventilation hood completely –I'll explain how that's done later in the series.

Chapter 6
The Silent River

It's pitch dark outside my tent and I am miles from the nearest human habitation. I was sleeping peacefully in my down bag but something has woken me up, although I don't know what. I lie for a few moments, listening. Silence. I begin to drift off, back into my cocooned world, when I hear a kind of groan. It must be a stag close by. It is bitterly cold on this March night and I reason it must have come down from the hills for shelter. I close my eyes again, and then there's a loud crack. I am fully awake now. No stag could make that noise. Something is out there. I roll over and fumble for my head torch, trying to decide what is making these noises. Another loud crack and the sound of something splintering. I fumble through my possessions but can't find the torch. A light from inside the tent and the sound of my movement will scare whatever it is away – if I can just find the torch. There is a loud creak that sounds as if it is right outside my tent. Adrenaline surges through me. My hand finds the torch, and I flood the tent with light and give a shout. There is another groan; whatever it is, it is still there.

A few months after my first trip with the tent in Gairloch, as temperatures plunge and weathermen forecast some of the coldest nights of the year, I decide to pack my tent and head for Achnasheen, about an hour's drive from Inverness. In pre-Covid days, I often spent nights at Inver mountaineering hut, a small cottage a couple of miles away from the Highland village. The hut has been closed due to restrictions for many months but, although I can't enter the building, there is nothing to stop me camping outside. With no one for miles, the risk from the virus is non-existent.

The hut is owned by the Jacobite Mountaineering Club, which is based in Edinburgh, and I keep an eye on the place when travel restrictions stop club members travelling this far north. My first visit during the pandemic had been in the summer, when travel restrictions were still in force. The guidance in force at the time allowed for visits for the purposes of maintenance, so I was permitted to drive the fifty or so miles to check the place over but forbidden to stay the night.

The first time restrictions allowed me to travel to the hut was in July. Having spent so long confined to my flat, it felt strange to drive into the hills again. For months I had only driven into town, restricted to a five-mile radius from my flat. Once my car accelerated past fifty miles per hour, the speed was scary. It took me fully half an hour to adjust to being able to drive at over thirty miles per hour. Seeing the countryside flashing past unnerved me.

When I was last in the hills it had been winter, before lockdown was imposed. The colours of the landscape then were muted browns and greys. When I returned, summer was in full flight and everywhere was a riot of green. It was as if there had been an explosion of trees, leaves and grass. Normally, I would watch as spring came and slowly morphed into summer, but the pandemic meant that this felt as if it had happened overnight. The familiar path from the layby and down the steps was so overgrown it was almost buried, showing how few people had walked this way in recent months. It was as though mankind had been removed from the landscape by some cataclysm and nature was returning.

When I come back in March, I am allowed to travel but not to visit the hut. It feels odd setting up my tent yards from a building I had often visited but which regulations now prevent me from entering. Obviously, as I am the only person for several square miles, there is nothing to prevent me from sneaking into the hut but I feel I am under a duty of trust not to do so. Having watched events since unfold, I am now sure that if I had been Boris Johnson I would have happily used the hut and invited a dozen folk round for a "business meeting" involving several crates of beer and wine, a game of British Bulldogs, and someone throwing up outside. I wouldn't do that; I have a conscience.

~

The hut sits on a small strip of land between two lochs; both are frozen solid. Even the stream which babbles past the hut is stilled by the cold, its waters under several inches of undulating ice, as if the stream has been frozen mid-flow by the magic spell of an ice witch. The ground is frozen iron hard and I struggle to drive the tent pegs in more than a few inches. As there is no wind, this doesn't worry me as I reason that even a few inches of this frozen ground will hold the pegs securely.

I'm becoming more proficient now at erecting the tent and making it wind- and weather-proof. After my experience in Gairloch, when the wind had done its best to lift the floor and fight its way into the tent, I purchased a set of groundsheet pegs. These are a little like large nails with a round plastic head about two centimetres across. They are designed so that you can drive them through the eyelets in the wall of the tent and hold it securely down. They won't be taking huge forces, so they only need to be around six centimetres long. The good thing about the plastic head is that if you happen to step on one, then it won't damage the tent or you.

I get my tent up just as darkness falls, then light my paraffin lamp and settle down for the evening. I have heard that a lot of folk don't like the idea of wild camping because they are uncomfortable in the countryside at night. They are afraid of the dark. That's understandable as most of us live in towns and cities where streetlamps and house lights mean true darkness is something we rarely experience and feels alien. Out in the hills, a night with no moon and low cloud can bring a deep darkness –an absolute absence of light that can be unnerving. Unless you have a torch, it is impossible to move.

Fear of the dark is perhaps more profound than merely our modern-day lack of familiarity with it. For thousands of years, primitive men spent their nights in the protective orbit of firelight, the flames warding off bears and wolves. Beyond the circle of firelight, danger lurked, and the darkness brought fear. Even over the last few hundred years some people have held very strong beliefs that the night was the realm of witches and evil spirits.

I look forward to the darkness. Perhaps because I have spent so many nights in bothies, I've lost my fear of the dark world. For me there is something special about being out in the hills at night. It can be magical to wander in the moonlight through a transformed landscape, listening to the hoot of an unseen owl. After dark many creatures that are hidden during the day emerge. Darkness is nature's domain and we are confined to the electric lights of our houses or to sitting behind the headlights of our cars. The darkness is a wild place –that's why I love it.

One of the great pleasures of this kind of camping is lighting the stove. Unlike bothy fires, the stove is easy to light. I place two or three firelighters, a little kindling and a couple of small logs in the mouth of the stove. I learnt from my previous expedition not to overload the stove with wood. One match and the bright yellow flames begin to dance. In minutes, the warm glow from the stove fills the tent and I can sit in comfort, reading and listening to music. It is hard to believe that on the other side of the canvas wall of the tent the temperature is well below freezing. I'm still struggling to prevent the stove turning the tent into a sauna. The heat is rising from the stove. What I am sitting in is called a hot tent for good reason; I know now why it hasn't been called a warm tent.

The tent has vents in the side, close to the floor, and others that are operated by a pulley system in the apex of the tent around the pole. When I first used the tent, I treated it as I would have all the other tents I have ever used, all the way from the great canvas monstrosity of an army tent to my two-man Vango. In cold weather I closed the vents and tried to keep the weather out. In the hot tent, I began to open the vents, largely to prevent myself from being cooked by the stove. The pulley system for the roof vents looked complicated but I began to realise it is actually simple. I pull on a cord and it opens one section of the vent in the roof. When I release the cord the elasticated cords on the outside of the tent pull it closed. This lets both the tent and me breathe, and allows me to regulate the temperature.

Condensation is the enemy of all tent dwellers in cold weather. The Safir 7 is a single-skin tent, something that made me wary of it at first. My experience of all single-skin tents is that the walls drip with condensation. There may be some high-tech tents with breathable walls but I've never stayed in one. I am beginning to understand that this tent works on different principles to the tents I've used before. It relies on being ventilated, so the stove can maintain an air current. The heat from the stove, and the convection currents of air this produces through the vents, means that moisture is carried out of the tent so condensation doesn't form. It has taken me a while to realise how this works. The hot tent has been more of a learning curve than I expected.

I spend a few hours enjoying my tent and experimenting with its vents before I climb into my sleeping bag and settle down for the night. It is about 3:00 a.m. when I begin to hear the strange groans and creaks outside the tent. I decide to leap out of bed to investigate. That is the plan. What happens is I find I am inextricably tangled in my sleeping bag, and the leap turns into a face plant, followed by a crawl, followed by fumbling around until I can eventually find my boots. I unzip the tent and shine my torch into the darkness.

The sounds are coming from near the stream. I can't imagine what is making them. Is a stag falling through the ice? I stumble towards the stream, and then I see it. The thick layer of ice that covered the stream is moving. Big sheets of ice are cracking and water is spouting into the air. It is then that I realise the sparkling frigid world I had gone to sleep in the previous evening is gone. The temperature must have risen twenty degrees overnight. The heaving sheets of ice that sparkle in my head torch beam are being lifted up by the rising stream as thawing ice from above swells its waters. The fickle Highland weather is capable of changing totally in only a matter of hours.

Returning to my tent, I find that several of the pegs have

thawed out of the ground and the tent is beginning to lean at an alarming angle. The iron-hard ground that resisted my efforts to hammer the pegs home yesterday is now soft and spongy. I shouldn't have given in so easily and should have known that a dramatic thaw was possible, no matter how unlikely that felt. Another lesson to note down.

Chapter 7
Camping in the Highlands

The Highlands of Scotland is a big place. I'm constantly surprised by the number of places I have yet to explore. I like to scour maps and seek out somewhere to camp. The more obscure it is, the less likely other folk have camped there and the more I enjoy it. I'm poring over OS maps one evening when I realise I've never been to Achiltiebuie, despite being close to it on a number of occasions, and it occurs to me this is something I should remedy. By all accounts, it is a spectacular area. The village is reached by driving north beyond Ullapool and turning west, off the main road, through a spectacular scenery of lochs and step mountains rising up from the sea. The population of the Coigach peninsula is 228, which gives you some idea of how empty the place is. The village occupies a thin ribbon of coastal land overlooking the Summer Isles at the foot of Ben More Coigach. The coast and islands have some of the best diving, sailing and kayaking anywhere in Scotland and have sheltered bays, sea caves to explore and clean sandy beaches.

Travelling to Achiltiebuie, I drive north and west and pass through the village of Ullapool, which is both a fishing harbour and a ferry port. The journey to Ullapool takes you through some open hill country populated by wide glens, deep lochs, and high hills. The country you pass through on the way to the small port is wild enough, but the nature of the country changes as soon as you pass through Ullapool, which has the feel of a frontier town. Beyond Ullapool the landscape changes. It becomes more rugged still, with the coastal road weaving its way between steep rock faces and a multitude of lochs, ranging from those no bigger than a small pond to open stretches of water several miles long.

As you leave Ross and Cromarty and pass north into Sutherland, the nature of the land changes. It is not simply that it is more rugged and even more sparsely populated than the rest of the Highlands, but there is a change in character that is difficult to define. This is a land on the edge of Britain. The very fringes of this island lie in these deep lochs and on this ragged coastline, places where the wind and the sea hold sway. Turning north, off the main road and on to the single-track road that follows the lochside, I begin to look for wild campsites, but the terrain is rough and there are few places I could easily camp. Soon, I am passing beneath Stac Pollaidh, a small hill that makes up for its lack of height by its jagged broken-toothed appearance, and is a spectacular hill despite its size. Even in the last ice age its summit stood proud and defiant above the glacier when most of the landscape was buried beneath hundreds of feet of ice.

As this is not an area I know well I could waste a lot of time looking for a wild camping spot, so I plan to head for the campsite at Altandhu, a few miles down the coast from the village. I don't usually use campsites but at least I'll have the luxury of showers and an easy pitch, with my car close at hand. The campsite sits just above a small, sandy bay and is elevated enough to get great views across to the Summer Isles. It's crowded with campervans and family tents but isn't quite full and has room for one wee tent, as I assure the woman taking my booking that I possess.

It's a warm evening with a gentle breeze and my canvas home is soon erected. The air is full of the sounds of children playing and the smell of burgers sizzling on barbeques. I'm headed to the nearest tap to fill my water carrier when disaster strikes.

As I pass a campervan, a cheery Yorkshire voice asks, "Have you come far?"

The voice belongs to a small, stout, middle-aged man, dressed in an overly large tee shirt and a pair of shorts big enough to house several elephants. He has a sun hat perched on his head with a dozen or so badges pinned to it.

He smiles at me when I look his way and repeats the question. "Has thou travelled far?"

He speaks in the kind of Yorkshire accent I remember well from my days in Barnsley.

It seems an innocent enough question, so I reply. "No, I live in Inverness. Not far."

I'm about to head back to my tent when he leaps forward

and places a hand on my shoulder. "Oh, I've been to Inverness, thou knows."

Then I make a fatal error: I respond with a question. "Really?"

It isn't much of a question. I haven't asked him when, or if he'd enjoyed it. It was barely a question at all, more of a statement, but it is all the opening he needs. He tells me how he got there, what the weather was like, and how disappointed he was not to see the Loch Ness monster, even though he doesn't believe in all that nonsense. He talks incessantly, as if he's been supplied with a surplus of words and has to give them away before he explodes. His language is spattered with "thee" and "thou" as though he is from the eighteenth century.

I grow acutely conscious that my life is ticking away and it feels like I'm wasting precious time listening to Norman. I want to run off, but somehow I can't. All the energy is being sucked out of me by this Yorkshireman. I can see my tent sitting less than a hundred yards away but it seems impossibly far. I yearn to be in it. How wonderful it would be to be sitting in my chair in silence! All that now seems just a distant dream. I look for a means of escape, but none appears.

"I'm on a strict diet, thou knows," he says, patting his overly large stomach.

I've no idea how he got on to the subject of food. I've not heard a word he's said since he began talking about the monster. I try to stroll away but he follows me. I may lose the will to live. I once encountered someone like him in a bothy who, in response to me asking him where he had been, took me literally and told me every hill he'd ever climbed, what the weather was like and how long it had taken him. Some people enjoy talking, or rather speaking, in complete ignorance of what the other person is feeling.

Norman is describing stopping for petrol at Tebay services on the M6 and giving me a detailed breakdown of the consistency of the sausage rolls when he is interrupted by another campervan dweller.

"Excuse me, I've made too many burgers," a tall man in a floral shirt announces, thrusting a plastic plate with several burnt fat-encrusted burgers piled on it towards us. "Help yourselves."

Norman takes two, but has no problem continuing to talk. "This bloke's in that funny tent."

Floral Shirt and Norman both seem to think this is hilarious.

"We've both got the same sort of van," Floral Shirt explains.

Norman beams, obviously glad to be joined by a fellow campervan dweller. "Actually, I have the slightly later model. They brought it out in the June of 2010," says Norman, spitting out bits of hamburger as he speaks.

Floral Shirt looks doubtful. "Are you sure?"

Norman is triumphant. "Mine has the modified toilet compartment. Three centimetres wider. Come and see."

Norman and Floral Shirt vanish into the campervan. I'm not the sort of person to miss an opportunity like this, so I leg it.

Sitting safely in my tent, I reflect on two things. Firstly, I wonder what kind of diet allows you to eat two burgers. I decide that whatever it is, I should be on it –the only problem being I'd need to eat more. The second thought I have is how grateful I am to not be obsessed by campervans. I would never want to be a nerd like Norman. Then I remember that I am writing a book about hot tents and my feeling of superiority evaporates. I have also remembered why I prefer wild camping over using campsites.

The following day, I dismantle my tent and escape. Achiltiebuie is a long ribbon of white houses dotted around a bay, overlooking the Summer Isles. Near the village there is a narrow strip of grass that would make a perfect campsite but, sadly, this is a fragile habitat, known in the west of Scotland as "machair". The very thin soil is composed of fragments of shell and is not able to withstand a great deal of traffic. For once, I can accept that the signs saying no camping have been erected here for a good reason. I take the small path that continues where the road ends and then winds steeply up the hillside of Ben Mor Ciogach. It's a warm day and I am relieved to reach the summit with its cooling breeze, and to be rewarded with stunning views across a patchwork of lochs, towards Stac Pollaidh on the far side of the hill and looking back towards the Summer Isles on the other. I decide that I must return to Achiltiebuie to find a suitable wild campsite in the area. There is so much to discover here and so much to see.

Chapter 8
Camping Tips

Some of you will be experienced wild-campers, having spent many nights in remote places. Other readers might be new to this new way of exploring wild places so I thought it might help if I passed on some of the things I've learnt. If you are camping wild in Scotland it helps to know a little about the laws relating to access. The law in Scotland relating to what you can and can't do in the countryside is very different to that in England. In Scotland, there is legislation broadly known as "the right to roam". Essentially, this means that you have the right to walk wherever you like. You can walk through fields and over hills, wander through woods and parkland, to your heart's content. This also includes having the right to stay overnight. In other words, you can camp or bivi where you like. This right is restricted to travelling under your own steam. Vehicular access is not allowed, although you'd be okay on a bike or in a canoe when there is no engine involved.

Camping in someone's garden would be pushing it too far.

As long as you are being reasonable, you won't get the local landowner hurling abuse at you and threatening to call the police while you brew your morning tea. This is very different to England, where you only have the right to walk on designated rights of way and certainly don't have the right to camp overnight. In England, many wild-campers talk about "stealth" camping; in other words, trying to get in and out of your camp spot without being detected. It is sad that someone who wants to spend a night out under the stars in a quiet spot has to resort the tactics of a cat burglar. Are we so determined to protect our rights to every square of the Earth that we're not using that we'll refuse to allow some poor soul even one night's sleep there? In one area of the Peak District, gamekeepers have been sent out at night with heat-sensitive cameras to detect the sleeping bodies of campers. At four in the morning they woke campers up and demand they move on. Just how desperate do you have to be to assert your rights that you are prepared to get someone to wake up some poor bloke sleeping in a tent in the middle of nowhere and shift him on?

It is certainly the case that some landowners in Scotland are less than welcoming towards hikers and campers, but our rights north of the border are enshrined in legislation. Hostile landowners can only try to deter public access. In some areas, mostly on sporting estates that adhere to the traditional sporting practices like driven grouse shooting, attempts to deter the public having access are subtle. Often, roads are fenced off in such a way as to make parking difficult.

Sometimes there are signs that say that shooting takes place all year round and that access is dangerous, which isn't true. I find walking on such estates unpleasant as I am so acutely aware of how much damage has been done to the environment and I find no joy in walking through a desolate killing ground.

Most of the time, I encounter no hostility and find people very welcoming, despite their incredulity at my desire to sleep in a tent in the depths of winter. Obviously, this only applies if you do no damage and don't cause any problems. Entering a building, such as a bothy, is a slightly different matter. It's taken for granted amongst the bothying community that you have a perfect right to spend the night in any remote open building you might come across in the hills, as long as it isn't locked. Most landowners also accept that principle. There are a great many open shelters across the Highlands that are used on a regular basis. Some are official bothies maintained by the Mountain Bothies Association, and some are simply buildings maintained by estates for the occasional use of shooting parties.

The sort of campsite I find ideal for my hot tent satisfies a number of criteria. Obviously, I'm looking for as flat a site as I can find. It may be something to do with the way I sleep. Even if there is only a slight slope, I wake up in the morning wedged against the side of the tent, having slowly rolled down hill during the night. I've never woken up outside the tent but it's only a matter of time. As well as being level, the ground where you set up your camp needs to be fairly even. In the

Highlands, much of the open ground is rough and covered in dense heather growth or very rough grass –known as tussock grass. This type of ground makes for poor camping as it will be almost impossible to get an even floor to the tent. I can see from the map where level ground is likely to be and, to an extent, how boggy it might be, but the OS map won't tell you if it is firm pasture or tussock grass. I like to plan where I am going, rather than spending ages driving up and down a glen trying to find a spot to camp in. One trick I have found invaluable in doing this is to use Google's Street View. This allows me to stand on the road and look at the ground I'm thinking of camping on. Street View gives me a lot of information that I can't get from a map, and I can usually get a really good idea of what sort of terrain to expect. The OS map will tell you that a track starts from the road at a particular point, but via Street View I can get a sense of what kind of track it is. Is it hardcore, is it deeply rutted, is it boggy or, as is sometimes the case in the Highlands, is it merely a figment of the cartographer's imagination?

Tracks are important to me because, if at all possible, I want to get as far away from the road as I can. This is my own idiosyncrasy. I don't like camping by the side of a road , despite the fact that many of the roads I use to explore the Highlands are quiet, single-track roads. Even in the summer, some of these roads may only have one car pass by every fifteen minutes. In winter, that frequency might drop to three or four cars per day. Remoteness is in the eye of the beholder. I often pass tourists who have stopped beside one of the

Highland's busiest roads, unfolded their tables and chairs, and sat down for a picnic. I have to remind myself that what I see as a busy highway appears to these folk to be a quiet rural road. They may live in the centre of Birmingham or London, in an environment constantly thronged with traffic noise. For them, my busy road is tranquillity itself. By the same token, when I camp five or six miles from the nearest house but only two hours' drive from my home and perceive it as a remote place, this might be considered over-crowded by a Siberian yak herder, used to being two weeks from the nearest solid dwelling.

The disadvantage of a hot tent is that it is heavy, around sixteen kilograms, and the stove is even heavier, close to twenty kilograms. These are not the sort of weights that you can carry very far in a backpack –not if you want to be able to stand up at the end of the day, that is. My solution to moving the tent has been to obtain a folding garden cart. The cart I chose has four broad wheels and is large enough to accommodate the stove and a few other accessories. It can also take the tent. It means that I can move my canvas home in about two trips. The ground more or less determines how far it is practical to pull the cart. On rough or soft ground the cart is hard to pull and so my journeys are short. On hard ground, like a hardcore Land Rover track, it's very easy to pull and I can travel further from the road. The manufacturers of the cart say its maximum load is one hundred kilograms. I never load it up with more than a third of that kind of weight. While the cart might be capable of carrying much more, the stress on the construction of the cart of moving that kind of weight would considerably shorten its life and make towing it feel like trying to pull a mountain.

It is possible to buy a carrying frame, which is like a seventies-style rucksack frame without the rucksack. This is to enable the more robust of us to carry the tent and the stove. I'm sure that in this way it would be possible to carry the tent anywhere you want although, unless you happen to be a Sherpa, this would be pretty strenuous. You would need to carry around twenty-five kilograms. That's possible, but not a comfortable load over any distance.

Weather conditions also play a part in choosing a good pitch. In winter, when winds might be strong, I try to find some shelter. In the summer, I look for places where there is likely to be a breeze to try to keep the midges at bay.

It's now quite common to find tracks and roadside pull-offs blocked off by either a chain or a line of boulders, the intention being to prevent campervans pulling off the road for a night or two. It is sad that landowners have felt the need to do this as the attitude in the Highlands to folk camping in vans used to be far more permissive. There are far fewer basic campsites than there were thirty years ago. Campsites have become larger and have much more luxurious facilities. The old-style campsites that were a farmer's field with a tap and a toilet have died out. It would be better if more places to camp that had simple facilities were made available. This would spread the load of visitors across the Highlands, giving villages that feel under pressure some respite and giving visitors greater choice. The chains and boulders are an advantage for me. My garden cart slips easily under the chains and no line of boulders can stop me. Effectively, all that these measures have done is to reserve these spots for folk like me who do not need to have vehicular access.

The great advantage of the hot tent is that you can camp all year round and be comfortable. I am as likely to go camping in January as I am in June. In fact, I prefer the cold, dark months. Sitting in the tent on a winter's evening, listening to hail bouncing off the canvas, warmed by the stove and basking in the light of a paraffin lamp is one of the best feelings I know. My experience is that, with a little knowhow –much of which I am trying to impart in this book –and with the right equipment, it is perfectly possible to enjoy camping throughout the year.

Chapter 9

The Sea Stag

Every time I turn off the main road between Fort William and Skye and take the long road to Kinloch Horn, I feel I have left most of the world behind. For the first few miles, the single-track road weaves its way through the deep green of the thick forest. I have to keep my eyes glued on the road ahead, ever watchful for a vehicle coming my way. I'm never very good at reversing but might have to back up a long way if I meet a larger vehicle coming towards me. This is complicated by the fact that my little Skoda is crammed with everything I'll need for the next few days. The biggest items I've packed are my tent, the stove, the garden cart for transporting everything about, my rucksack full of clothes, and my folding kitchen. There also seems to be an endless supply of smaller things I need to find space for in the car. Tinned food. Fresh food. Whisky. My folding chair, a kettle and pans, a washing-up bowl, and fuel for the stove. A myriad of little items climb into my car until I can no longer see anything in the rear-view mirror. This all adds to my dread of having to reverse more than a few feet, so I dash from passing place to passing place, always hoping that it'll be the other driver who has to go backwards.

These small roads can be treacherous and unforgiving, especially if you are not used to driving in such remote places where the roads are frequently too narrow to allow two cars to pass. Despite the low level of traffic, there is a high rate of accidents. One reason for this is simply the scenery. You turn a bend and there before you is a towering mountain, so it can be hard not to look.

Once, I was driving towards Glen Coe and couldn't pull my eyes from the summits. There was a car ahead of me but he was a long way ahead on the straight, fast road so I paid him little heed. My eyes were following the line of a route I had planned for the following day on a sharp ridge leading to the rocky summit. I glanced back at the road and, to my horror, the rear of the car in front, so distant only a moment ago, was only three feet from my bonnet. I couldn't stop in time, so hurled my car to the other side of the road, missing the other vehicle by inches. What I hadn't realised when I saw him in the distance was that the driver was also enjoying the view and had slowed to a crawl. I once encountered the worst-case scenario on a Highland single-track road and found myself screeching to a halt, with the radiator grill of an articulated lorry bearing down on me. On that occasion we had both been enjoying the view and relying on the fact that the Highland roads are frequently empty in winter. We exchanged embarrassed glances after we'd stopped, both of us knowing we should have been paying more attention to the road. Seeing the four-wheel drive teetering on the edge of the road brings back those memories. I slow down for the rest of the journey and make sure my eyes remain on the road.

After a few miles, the road emerges from the forest and then follows the northern edge of Loch Choich. By the time I am a few miles from my campsite, the only other travellers on the road are a few bored-looking Highland cows who stand blocking the road. These are huge beasts and they make it clear that they will move out of my way when they decide it is time. I will have to wait. A cow stares at me from beneath a huge ginger fringe, its massive horns emphasising the size of its great shaggy head. Enormous brown eyes regard me with disdain. I am just another human in one of those infernal metal boxes that bother a girl when she's trying to digest her grass. The cows look fearsome, but they are gentle giants. They could be formidably aggressive if they wanted to, but one thing stops them –they simply can't be bothered. After returning my gaze for a few moments, the great shaggy beast takes a few languid steps to the side of the road. She moves just enough, and no more, for me to squeeze my little Skoda past her. She's letting me know that this is her road and that I should be grateful that she is happy to move at all. I suppose she lives here, after all.

Twenty minutes later, I am wandering around a field with a small wooden disc in my hand, looking for just the right place to put it down. This moment is important because the circle of wood I have in my hand will mark the centre of my temporary home for the next few days. I enjoy erecting this tent now, which is something I never thought I'd say. I must have put up hundreds of tents in my life but I wouldn't say it was something I had previously looked forward to. This tent is different. I no longer struggle with unfamiliar bits of canvas and tangled guy lines as I did on my first campsite at Gairloch. Now, I have a system and a well-rehearsed routine that I actually enjoy. I once read a book called *Zen and the Art of Motorcycle Maintenance* –this is Zen and the art of tent erection. I find my central spot, anchor the wooden plate and begin to set out the pegs. The tent is octagonal in its footprint and the plate has lines on it that I follow with a tape that shows me where each peg needs to go. I end up with a circle of pegs around my central point. Then I bring the tent to the pegs, hook the eight corner pegs, grab the central pole and charge in like a medieval spear-chucker, putting the pole in place and lifting up the tent. In seconds, my temporary home takes shape.

This is one of my favourite places to camp; I call it the monkey puzzle campsite because of the monkey puzzle tree standing beside a small rectangle of pines a hundred yards away. I'm two hundred yards from the quiet single-track road which even now, at the height of summer, has only one or two cars per hour ride its roller coaster into the hills. The babbling stream I'm camped beside runs into a small, reed-fringed loch and all around this amphitheatre rocky peaks rise into the sky. My campsite is at the centre of a huge rock bowl. I'm not very good at judging the size of anywhere in units of football pitches, as is often done. I've never been a football fan so find it difficult to say how big a pitch is. Perhaps you could fit twenty football pitches into this secluded area. This campsite feels right for me. It's sheltered by the rock walls and is level enough to be comfortable. A tumbledown ruined cottage sits just across the road. I have set my tent up on an area of flat ground which has obviously been cleared of boulders and bracken. I wonder if the area of flat ground I have set my tent up on was once cultivated by the people who lived in that old ruin. Perhaps they grazed their sheep here or grew potatoes. As I put down the rugs on the floor of my tent and unfold the wire shelves of my kitchen I sense a peace in the place, as if it was once a home and welcomes me back as a trusted friend.

There is little wind today, so the tent stands without me needing to tighten up the guys. This is good because it allows me to attach the floor with ease. I've perfected installing the floor although I had a real battle with it when I first did it. The process is actually simple. I slide the floor under the central pole then attach each corner of the floor, making sure I peg the groundsheet down as I pass each corner. Then I tighten the guys and the tent takes shape before me. It is a stark contrast to many of the lightweight nylon tents I've erected, where you find yourself engaged in a geometrical battle with poles that need to slide through sleeves and locate in tension pockets; the poles never quite want to go where you want them to go and I've often found myself trying to force a pole into some little pocket.

After an hour or so of unpacking and two or three runs back to my car with the garden cart to fetch my tent and its furniture, I sit in the open doorway of my shelter and watch a pair of buzzards as they circle back and forth across the cliffs before me, their sharp cries echoing off the rock face. This August evening is warm and the breeze is gentle. I decide I'll not unpack the wood-burning stove. I'll be warm enough without it. Later that evening, as the sun goes down and the heat of the day subsides, I feel a sense of incredible peace inside the canvas walls of my tent. The only sound is the babbling of the small stream only feet from my tent. There is something soothing in the sound of the water tumbling endlessly over the pebbles. I decide that I'll always make an effort to camp close to moving water if I can; it is a natural backdrop. I find myself sitting content in the warm glow of my old paraffin lamp, looking forward to the day to follow.

The following morning, the day dawns bright. I cook my porridge on the small gas stove, make up a few sandwiches and take the short drive to where the public road ends. My plan is to take the coastal path that follows the shoreline to Barrisdale bothy. The bothy is not one maintained by the Mountain Bothies Association. It is one run by the estate. They charge five pounds to spend the night in this simple dwelling. It must be almost thirty years since I walked this coastal path and made my way to the bothy with a small group of friends. Here I am again, older but I suspect not wiser.

The road narrows and steepens as it descends to the head of

the sea loch. The sky is dotted with white clouds and even now the warmth of the August sun is making itself felt in the steep-sided glen. Ahead of me lies a great fjord, its waters shimmering blue, snaking out between the green of the steep-sided hills that plunge into the depths. I pass the café, which displays a large hardboard sign with the word "closed" painted on it in crude red letters. I remember passing a sign advertising the café twenty-two miles away, where the single-track road that ends here left the main road. There had been nothing to indicate that the café was closed on that sign. That's typical of the Highlands. If you decided it might be fun to visit this remote café for lunch you would have had a forty-four-mile drive for nothing. The assumption, presumably, is that if you have nothing better to do than visit the café in the first place, you won't mind wasting the best part of the day driving there only to discover that it has been shut for the better part of three months. It's a nice drive, after all.

As I park my car in the small car park, three older men sail around the headland in Canadian canoes. Their canoes are packed with serious-looking waterproof containers and each of the three boats is carrying a good load of supplies. I'm lacing my boots up when they land and begin to unload their canoes onto the beach. A small, elderly grey dog cautiously steps off one of the canoes and begins to make his way towards me. I trip over him as he steps in front of me for a quick trouser sniff.

"Sorry about him," one of the weather-beaten men calls over to me, his arms laden with plastic bags full of empty beer bottles. "He's blind, you see."

I do see, although obviously the dog doesn't. Part of me wants to make a comment that "Old Blind Dog" might be a good name for a pub, but I realise that my passion for one-liners is sometimes misplaced. When I gently move him out of the way with my hand, his tail wags in greeting to my touch.

I'm curious about these men. They look as if they have been out for several days and there is a professionalism about the way they have stowed their gear. Each canoe has a high-backed seat, which is something I've not seen before –perhaps a concession for these older guys.

"Been out long?" I ask.

The dog's owner smiles from beneath his bushy white beard. "Three days camping."

"You can get a fair amount of gear in those canoes." I'm beginning to wonder if this might be another way for me to get around with the hot tent.

He looks at me apologetically. "Well, we're all over seventy now. Not into roughing it, you see."

I can see he's a little embarrassed about all the equipment the group has. "Yes, you're right. I like to have a bit of comfort these days. I have a hot tent up the glen."

This piques the boatman's interest. "Have you? We wondered about one of those."

"You could get one in your canoes no bother," I explain. "I've a stove that keeps me warm at night."

"A stove!" he exclaims. "That sounds great."

"And I can stand up in the morning to put my trousers on."

He closes his eyes, savouring the concept of such unbridled luxury for men like us, of a certain age.

"You've each got a canoe? Is it not tricky handling one of those single-handedly at sea?" My canoeing experience is very limited, but I know enough to know that it is much more difficult to control a Canadian canoe alone than with a partner. A solo canoeist can only paddle on one side of the craft and it's a constant problem, especially if there is any kind of wind or swell, to keep it straight.

The canoeist dumps a large watertight container onto the beach and stands for a moment, unzipping his yellow waterproof jacket as the effort begins to overheat him. "Two of us were senior canoe instructors, you see."

"Ah, so you know what you're doing."

He laughs at this, with a great gap-toothed smile. "We like to think so. Like our creature comforts now though." He pats the barrel affectionately.

The blind dog is back, sniffing my ankles and wagging his tail. I bend to stroke him. They are only a few years older than me but there are not many senior citizens who could do what they do. I wonder if I'll be able to do what they are doing when I am their age.

"Good to get out." I smile and we share a secret moment, each knowing that infirmity is knocking at the door.

"Aye, it is." He glances at my walking poles. "You walking into Barrisdale?"

"Yes, that's it," I say confidently. Then with a little more honesty. "Well, maybe."

We laugh together, both knowing that the ambitions of old men and their abilities are frequently different things. As I begin my walk, the old dog follows close at my heels, maintaining his interest in my trousers, until he is called back by the canoeist.

Soon the track narrows, and I walk along a thin line between the cliffs rising above me to my left and the sea only a few feet to my right. Below me, the rock drops sheer for a few feet into the water. The sunlight is penetrating deep below the surface, and in the blue-green murk of the water I can see crabs scuttling about and small fish living out their lives. Ever since I went fishing as a small boy with my father, the secret world that lurks beneath the water's surface has always fascinated me. It's a world separated from ours by only the thin veil of the water's surface. So close, and yet so alien that we can only spend the briefest of times in it. The scent of the sea fills the air, intoxicating me with the sense of this place, teeming with life.

I have to stand for some minutes, taking in the scene. This is a perfect place, as perfect a moment as it is possible to get. The breeze is gentle and warm, the air buzzes with insects, and life abounds everywhere. The hills sweep in great curves like some gigantic sea, frozen in a moment of time. I can't understand why I haven't been back here for so long –how could I forget this place? Life distracted me and now, in retirement, I have the gift of time to go wherever the fancy takes me.

After a mile or so, the steepness of the high ground eases and the hills lean back a little. I'm scanning the beach when a stag rises from the heather, only feet from me. I expect him to run but he stands, watching me with his deep brown eyes. He is a young stag, perhaps a year old. Seaweed dangles in bunches from his antlers, giving him a bizarre appearance, as if he has been decorated for some strange event. In the rut, stags will sometimes tangle their antlers with small branches and twigs to make them look more impressive, but that time of year is a month away. I can only think he has been feeding on seaweed. I have never been this close to a stag before. Even the semi-tame animals fed through the winter on sporting estates to keep their numbers artificially high wouldn't tolerate a human being this close. He watches me, cautious but unafraid. When an animal behaves so oddly it is often injured or sick but he appears healthy. Perhaps eating seaweed has driven him mad. I pass by and he watches me without any sign of fear. A strange, memorable encounter in this lonely place.

Soon the path begins to climb and, as it does so, the heat of the day begins to build. Huge dragonflies buzz past me, like helicopters out on patrol. I climb the first hill on the route to Barrisdale and find myself slowing down. I have never enjoyed walking in hot weather and find myself increasingly feeling as if I want to sit and simply admire the view. This coastal walk is possibly one of the best in Scotland; its views are spectacular and its remoteness gives it a unique aspect. I wonder why I have not been back here for so long. The hot tent has given me a freedom to explore such places afresh. I have a portable base that I didn't have before.

I sit in the heather and enjoy the sandwiches I had made earlier in the tent. Today is Monday. Even in this Covid pandemic, all across Britain people are climbing into cars and heading into work or sitting in front of computers to apply themselves to endless tasks. I feel incredibly privileged to enjoy the health and freedom that retirement has brought me. I still expect that a bloke with a clipboard will turn up at any moment and tell me that this has all been an awful mistake and that I need to report for work tomorrow morning. He'll have a huge backlog of tasks that I should have been completing over the last few years. Even worse than that, and my greatest fear of all, there'll be a meeting I need to attend where some mindless bore will drone on for hours about where we have all gone wrong. He'll have a PowerPoint presentation which he'll proceed to flash up on a screen and then read word for word, on the assumption that none of those present are able to read. I'll turn away from the screen and subtly glance out of the window, longing to be gone, like I did for forty years or so. I probably wasn't in the same meeting for forty years; it just felt that way.

Today, I can sit enjoying my cheese sandwiches and I am free to do anything I like, or nothing at all if I want to. It's like somebody slipped me a golden key and I made it out of the door.

As I eat, the sun rises in the sky and the heat of the day grows. I always wilt in the heat. When the temperature gets into the mid-twenties my ability to function ceases. I seek the shade and can only sit, quietly sweating, until the sun goes down and life can begin again. It's barely credible that there are people who seek the sun. They get on a plane and fly somewhere they know it's hot and then go and lie on a beach in the sun! I can barely credit it.

When it's hot, my neighbours say, "Isn't the weather wonderful? You must be enjoying getting out in the hills."

No, I'm not. Walk up a Highland hill in the heat and you'll sweat. After a while you'll crave water and find yourself gasping by a stream. Then the clegs (the Highland name for horseflies) will get you, sinking their sharp fangs into your moist, pink flesh. It's unbelievable to me that there are people who will go onto a beach and willingly expose their skin to the enemy. They want to get burnt –that's like a sausage wanting to be cooked. I don't go to the beach. I hide under a tree, cover my body in factor-one-thousand sun cream and sulk until it goes dark. Only then do I emerge, like some hill-walking vampire, basking in the moonlight.

I head back to my tent. Sadly, the café is still closed and the ice cream I had dreamt of, a slice of sweet winter, is denied me. Back at my tent I enjoy a cup of tea and decide that, being only yards from a small loch, I really ought to do some fishing. I have brought with me an old split cane fly rod that once belonged to my father, who loved fishing as much as life itself. When I touch the cork handle and run my fingers down its smooth varnished wood, I feel a connection with him beyond words. I pass the afternoon hurling a fly into the water of the loch. As usual, I catch nothing. I don't expect to –I am not the expert angler he was. Catching a fish doesn't matter to me. What I enjoy is standing beside the water in this peaceful place and holding his fishing rod, doing something he would have enjoyed beyond measure.

The next morning, I decide to climb the steep path that leads up into the hills behind the tumbledown ruined cottage sitting across the narrow single-track road from my campsite.

The path up from the glen is steep and uncompromising, rising in a series of short zigzags. I am soon looking down upon my temporary home. The path is a joy. It is instantly obvious that this is an old path, one that has carried feet over these hills for hundreds, perhaps thousands, of years. Scotland abounds with paths that were planned and constructed, drawn on a map by the planner's pen. These planned paths never feel the same as the old routes. This path was not designed, it evolved. It weaves its way up through the short cliffs in sympathy with the landscape. Shepherds made this path moving their sheep to higher pasture. Ghillies made this path carrying the carcasses of stags down the hill on sturdy footed garrons. Lovers made this path, walking to assignations in distant glens. Each footfall tells me this. The path is tuned to the rhythm of a walking man.

Just below the ridge, I pause and take a drink from a small stream. Already I can see the glen winding its way through distant hills off to the east on the road I drove only a few days ago. Climbing higher still, I catch the breeze and find myself marvelling that even in the height of the summer season I can see no other human being in the landscape. Even when I take out my binoculars and scan the summits, they are empty. Out of the heat of the valley, the cool breeze draws me on and upwards towards the summit of this hill.

I stop for a moment, sweating a little and panting, waiting to catch my breath, and a woman in her early twenties appears over some rocks as she makes her way down the hill.

"Hello! Nice day," she calls, as she passes the old man struggling for breath. I realise I am dishevelled. The climb has taken its toll on me. She looks as though she has just strolled to the corner shop to buy some milk. Her hair is in place and there is not even a hint of moistness on her skin. She looks as though she has never shed a drop of sweat in her life.

She reminds me of a couple I once saw when I was walking part of the Great Glen Way. Sometimes I take the bus to Drumnadrochit, west of Inverness, along Loch Ness. From the Highland village I can walk back over the hills to my home, around eighteen miles away. Once I noticed two runners on the bus, a man in his early forties and a woman almost half his age. I couldn't help but hear their conversation. The older man was treating the woman to all his knowledge and experience about running ultra-marathons, something he seemed to know a great deal about. He was telling her what to eat and how to pace herself over the long distances she would face. She sat listening attentively but leaning back a little. He was sat a little too close to his female companion and looked to me to be very keen to impress her.

I got off the bus in Drumnadrochit and they carried on,

obviously intending to run over twenty miles back to the Highland capital. I didn't see them again until I had walked all but the last two miles back home. I was sitting, sore-footed and gathering myself for the last leg of the walk, when the girl passed me. She was gliding over the ground, enjoying every footstep as she effortlessly jogged home. She smiled and waved as she left me in her wake and looked as if she could have turned and run the whole route again with infinite ease. One hundred yards behind was her older suitor. He could no longer run. He was managing to move forward in a controlled stagger. Only half of his body seemed capable of movement. He made progress by hurling one arm in front of him and then trying to catch it up with the rest of his body. He looked as though he had already suffered several strokes and was waiting for the final heart attack. The agonised expression on his face made me think of someone whose genitals have been trapped in a vice for a very long time with the release button just out of reach.

He was learning a very important lesson that I learnt long ago. It doesn't matter how much experience you have, how many times you've done it before: nothing beats being twenty-two and weighing four stone less.

From the top of the hill, I look down into the glen and can just make out the yellow cone of my tent sitting on the valley floor beside the waters of the loch, far below. Now I can look down on the forest that stood beside the loch and I notice that the first few brushstrokes of autumn were beginning to paint the trees a golden brown. Summer is ending and autumn will soon be upon us. My home lies down there, in the field beside the loch, in that canvas shelter. I stand in the breeze wondering what lies before me, beyond this season in the nomadic home I am learning to love.

Book 2
Lessons from the Wood

I shall be telling this with a sigh
Somewhere ages and ages hence:
Two roads diverged in a wood, and I—
I took the one less travelled by,
And that has made all the difference.

Robert Frost

Chapter 10
Loch Arkaig

Some special places inspire the imagination and take you to a different world. These locations vary for all of us. One such place for me is Loch Arkaig, a great ribbon of water that stretches west from a spot not far from Fort William and heads into remote hills. The glen forks beyond the end of the loch, some eleven miles from the hydro dam that raised its level thirty years ago. The southern branch leads on into Glen Pean where there is a remote bothy. From there you can trek west, through the rugged narrows of the glen and on to the shores of Loch Morar. This loch, with a depth of just over 1,000 feet, is the deepest body of water in Britain and has its own legendary monster. The northern branch follows the River Dessary to where a high pass leads on to Sourlies, a tiny coastal bothy, on the doorstep of the rugged bounds of the Knoydart peninsula.

Glen Dessary captured my imagination when I first backpacked there with my two old friends, Martin and Joe. Those of you who have read my first book, *The Last Hillwalker*, will remember them from our teenage foot-slogging adventures. I still recall cresting a ridge and looking down into the broad green glen below. For a young man from Merseyside the place was impossibly remote and wild beyond my imagination.

I have visited these hills many times, walking the summits, staying in the lonely bothies and camping in the glens, and now I am drawn to them again. There are legends that Jacobite gold was buried here in the aftermath of the rebellion. I'm not sure if that legend is true but I can tell you for certain that there is a secret box stashed in the glen, full of food and whisky. I know that because I stashed it a few years ago. Sadly its whereabouts are now as much a mystery to me as the rebel gold. Perhaps some lost hillwalker will find it one day.

It is late September when I cram my hot tent into the back of my black Skoda and head along the road beside Loch Ness, with plans to camp next to Loch Arkaig. The weather map is spotted with raindrops and predicts "showers." Anyone who travels the Highlands will know that the term "showers" can have any number of meanings. A shower can be the briefest of moist squalls, barely wetting the hood of your cagoule, or it can herald several days of incessant rain. A shower can last a week and cause minor flooding. By the same token, if the forecast says "heavy rain" it's probably a good idea to invest in a wetsuit.

Once I regarded the autumn as a dead period. Too wet to hill walk, too warm for the joys of winter. I rarely went into the outdoors and simply sat at home waiting for the first signs of winter. The hot tent has changed that. I'm now determined to go out in all kinds of weather and to learn to cope with whatever the Highlands has to throw at me. I want to know how to adjust to the seasons and learn how to live in wild places.

Living a nomadic existence is in our genes. For most of human history, we have travelled in makeshift shelters made of animal hide and supported by wood or the bones of large animals. That's how it has been for ninety-seven per cent of our history. It has only been for the last three per cent of our existence on Earth that we domesticated plants and animals, and our population numbers were able to explode. We slowly became fixed in one place and created our own urban environments. What we think of as a normal existence is very far from that. We are by nature nomads, so perhaps I need to rediscover that roaming spirit and free myself of the tyranny of bricks and mortar. That means embracing every season and all kinds of weather. I don't think I'll give up my flat. I'm not ready to abandon the central heating and widescreen TV just yet, although it is something I've thought about. I want to spend as much time as I can outdoors. I'm going to have to get used to a little rain.

Driving down the A82 beside Loch Ness, I watch the clouds gathering grey above the deep water of this great lake. There is a statistic about Loch Ness that I still find hard to comprehend: there is more water in this twenty-two-mile loch than in all the lakes of England and Wales combined. That's a hell of a lot of water. There are 263,000 million cubic feet of it sitting below the surface. How anyone worked that out is a mystery to me, but it does tell you a lot about just how vast this inland body of water is. Loch Ness never freezes over; it's too big for even the coldest winter to make much impression on the temperature of the water. In summer, the first few feet of the loch do warm up but a swimmer splashing around and churning the water up will soon feel the chill of cold water from the depths.

I call into the supermarket in the village of Drumnadrochit for a sandwich. Covid-19 is a still a threat and all the folk shopping in the mini-supermarket are wearing masks. As I slip mine on, I wonder how long this crisis will continue.

I look across the loch, beyond the village and towards Boleskine where the ruins of Aleister Crowley's house still stand. Crowley was a notorious occultist and writer, and he was also a mountaineer. I am fascinated by the man and performed a one-man play about him in the 2010 Edinburgh Fringe. The house burnt down a few years ago and a trust are now trying to raise funds to restore the place. I'm hoping to get a chance to look around the ruins. I have an irrepressible urge to recite the words of Crowley's famous ritual, aimed at summoning the god Horus, in the very place where the man himself recited them. It's well over one hundred years since those words were spoken in that house. I'm certain of one thing: if I do manage to summon a demon, I'll be out of there before you can blink.

One hour later I am driving through a narrow steep-sided glen, a place so overhung with trees that it is often dark and gloomy even on the brightest of days. This is the Mile Dorcha, or dark mile, that marks the entrance to this hidden glen. Today, with grey clouds obscuring the sun, this place is even gloomier than usual. Even though it isn't raining, water drips down from the trees where the mist has condensed, giving the dimly lit glen a dank atmosphere. Beyond this narrow glen lies the start of the loch, with the narrow road hugging the shore and the waters of the loch lapping at the edge of the tarmac. This is Loch Arkaig's secret trap. In periods of heavy rain, and these are frequent here, the loch rises and floods the road, trapping people in the glen. It's usually possible to drive through the flood if you have a big enough vehicle with four-wheel drive, but if you were driving an average car, there would be nothing left to do but sit and wait for the waters to subside. If it keeps raining, you could be trapped for days by the floodwater.

Another trick that the loch can perform is that it can flood even when it has stopped raining and the risk of flooding appears to be over. This happens because the rivers and streams in the hills can still be pouring water into the loch for hours after the rain ceases. Martin, Joe and I were caught by the rising water a few years ago. We had spent a cosy night in Glen Pean bothy, at the far end of the loch. All night the wind had raged, and the bothy was battered by ceaseless rain hurled against its walls in the storm. The following morning the weather was quiet and dry. The storm of the previous day seemed only a memory and we relaxed as we drove down the loch, heading back to my home in Inverness. Our mood changed abruptly when we turned a corner and found the road under three feet of water.

We decided we had no choice but to abandon the car and scramble round the hillside. Halfway round, we discovered a couple of locals driving through the flood. One was managing to get through in a small van. They told us that the loch was dropping fast and if we waited an hour or so, we should be okay to drive through. An hour later I decided to risk it and made the perilous drive through the water. There were a few hairy moments when I did not know if I was driving on the road or in the loch. At one point I thought I was in big trouble when waves broke over the bonnet. The flooded section was only 200 yards –but it was one of the longest drives of my life.

Aside from the floods, this area is a bothy-goer's paradise. There is Glen Pean bothy, where the three of us weathered the storm. Just on the other side of the hill, and easily accessible, is Achiu bothy. This bothy tends to be popular as it is used as a stop-off point on the Cape Wrath Trail. As well as these two bothies, there are at least another three or four which are accessible, with varying degrees of leg work, from the head of Loch Arkaig.

From the mouth of the loch, just beyond the end of the Dark Mile, it is a short walk to Invermallie bothy. This bothy is at risk from the rising waters of the loch. One evening I spent a night there and got chatting to two Munroists who travelled up every weekend to the Highlands from their homes in Yorkshire. That night we talked about hillwalking gear, and they told me about Paramo wet weather clothing. They were so enthusiastic that I resolved to buy some –a decision I have never regretted. The following morning, I made my way down the steep wooden stairs and was alarmed to see my boots wandering past the bottom of the staircase without me. The loch had risen during the night and there was a foot and a half of water covering the ground floor.

My companions and I waded out, and found the bothy surrounded by several hundred yards of fast-flowing water. This added interest to the walk out of the bothy as we all had to be very careful not to stray off the submerged track into deeper water. I was reduced to shuffling along, poking my poles into the water to feel for the track beneath. I felt as though I was walking through a river. Those two incidents have left me with considerable respect for Loch Arkaig's ability to surprise the unwary.

Today I follow the road around the loch, driving through the immense greenery of the forest which tumbles down the hillside and all the way to the water's edge. After a few miles I arrive at a series of shacks by the waterside. There are caravans and tents with bits of wood tacked on to make improvised extensions –the holiday homes of eccentrics who rent these waterside plots from the estate, spending most of their summers fishing the loch. This is the tiny community of folk who fish the loch.

Round a bend, I find two of the fishermen struggling to reverse a trailer carrying a boat into their campsite. They are both in their early sixties. One of them approaches me, apologising for blocking the road. He is wearing an ancient drysuit and sporting wild, white flowing locks. He gives me a gap-toothed grin when I explain to him that I'm in no hurry and the delay is no problem.

"Have you been fishing today?" I ask.

He shakes his head sadly. "Aye, nothing at all. Not so bad yesterday. It's this weather."

I look up to see great grey clouds rolling menacingly across the sky. It is much warmer than it should be at this time of year. "Yes, it's odd weather."

He nods. "It *is* odd weather. I've been cooking in this suit."

The drysuit he is wearing looks to be several layers deep.

"I've just come from Inverness. It's really warm there."

He nods again. "Not natural. Colder tomorrow, though. This warm weather won't last."

As anywhere else in the UK, the state of the weather and the possibility of rain are sources of endless conversation. I decide that he must know if there are any campsites I can use.

"I'm looking for somewhere to camp."

He nods again; it's something he does a lot. "Yes, you can camp just past here. There's a wee promontory. You can have a fire."

"I don't need a fire. I've a hot tent," I explain.

He looks like the sort of man who would know what a hot tent is, but he looks puzzled.

"It's a tent with a wood-burning stove."

"How come it doesn't burn down?" he asks, looking as if he does not quite believe me.

"Come and see when I've got it up."

"I will." His grin exposes his gapped teeth as he nods some more. Eventually his companion manages to reverse the trailer through the narrow gate and I say goodbye.

He is right. There is a good parking place off the road, and a narrow path leads to a great campsite on the tiny peninsula that juts out into the loch. There is a flat area amongst the trees just big enough for the Tentipi. I haul my tent over and test the ground. This is a popular place to camp: the grass has been worn away and there is only bare earth crisscrossed with tree roots left. The air smells of rain and leaves. The wind picks up and I scan the dark clouds anxiously, wondering if I will get my tent up before the inevitable rain arrives. The ground is hard and the soil shallow but, to my surprise, the pegs for my tent sink in easily. I've learnt that any tent is only as good as its anchors. The weather forecast didn't mention wind but the weather here often ignores the forecast. I take no chances and make sure the tent is well anchored.

By some freak chance I get the tent up and secure seconds before bullet-like drops of rain begin to cascade down from the sky. The evening is still uncharacteristically warm for this time of year. I decide not to light the stove but to rely on my two paraffin lamps to heat the tent. Together they give off enough heat to keep the tent comfortable, although I'm always wary of having two lamps lit in the small space. They light the tent beautifully. The Duplex lamp gleams, and I take a pride in polishing the brass until it sparkles. The Duplex makes no noise but the Tilley, which is pressurised, hisses reassuringly. It's hard to say which produces the most light but they are both effective lights, and so much more atmospheric than an electric light. Even though a battery-operated torch would be simpler to light and less likely to get broken, I prefer the paraffin lamps as they transport me to a different age.

The problem with heating the tent with the lamps is that, even though they give off plenty of heat, they also produce carbon monoxide which means I need to be careful with them. I set up my carbon monoxide detector and am reassured by its small blinking light.

All night the rain pounds on the tent so heavily that I keep waking up. At one point I find myself coughing convulsively. Lying in the darkness, I decide it must be Covid-19. I try to think back to where I could have caught the virus and decide that it must have been the young woman who served me the Mexican chicken roll in the village of Drumnadrochit. She must have breathed on my sandwich and sealed my fate. What a cruel end, to be killed by a sandwich.

By morning my cough has gone and in the light of day it appears that my survival is less in doubt than it had been in the darkness of the night. I'm not sure what caused the coughing in the night but I am suspicious that it may have been spending the evening with both paraffin lamps burning. The rain eases a little and I drive to the section of road I know is likely to flood if the loch rises much higher. If it looks like it is going to flood, I will need to make a quick exit to avoid being trapped. When I arrive at the end of the loch, the water is lapping over the tarmac but it is only slightly higher than it was before. It seems that there is no imminent danger of being marooned so I return to my tent to brew tea and make my breakfast.

While I am sitting drinking tea the rain stops –well,

almost. I sit in the door of my tent and contemplate the world. From the narrow peninsula I can see the water of the loch through the trees. The place is green and lush, smelling of moss and the damp mustiness of the changing year. It is early in this autumn so, even though the breeze tumbles a few russet leaves past the tent flap, the trees are mostly still in leaf although the green hues are beginning to fade. I enjoy the shelter they offer me. I'm pleased to have found this campsite. It will be a good place to come to in winter when the high hills are frozen. I'll be able to sit here when the loch is still and the land is silent in the early frosts of December. I silently add this place to my list of wild campsites. I have half a dozen or more on my list now, and I am sure that I'll find many more as I explore the Highlands with my tent.

Last night was by far the wettest night I have had in my new tent. I was dry inside but the hours of pounding rain have left the canvas soaked. I realise that my decision not to light the stove was a mistake. The stove is the engine of this Tentipi. It keeps you warm in winter but can also drive out moisture in wet conditions. The lamps kept me warm but they couldn't push back against the deluge.

After my breakfast, I set up the stove.

I'm just about to light it when a voice greets me from outside the tent: "Well, I thought we'd better come and see this tent with a stove."

The two fishermen have brought folding chairs and in minutes we are sitting in the open tent chatting. I put a match to the stove and open the vents in the tent. After a few minutes, steam rises from the canvas as it begins to dry. The kettle boils quickly, and the three of us enjoy the first of several cups of tea while I listen to their stories.

The fishermen tell me that they have been fishing Loch Arkaig for over twenty years. They both live in Glasgow but head north every chance they get and practically live here in the summer.

We discuss the possibility of the road flooding. Dougie, the gentleman with the white hair and toothless grin, is an expert on the loch. "You'll be alright getting your car out for the rest of today, but there's rain coming tomorrow and you might be in trouble then."

His companion, Dave, has a short goatee beard. He draws on an elaborately carved pipe. "We've four-wheel drives, you see –better ground clearance than your Skoda. It'll no bother us."

The weather forecast and the dark, threatening clouds filling the sky tell me that more rain is imminent over the next few days. If Loch Arkaig hasn't burst its banks yet, it's likely to soon. The fishermen tell me that they can remember the road being closed by floodwater many times –for as long as ten days.

Although I had hoped to spend a few nights here, but I don't want to get trapped by floodwater and have to spend several days waiting for however long it takes it to recede. I decide I'll pack up and return home.

The fishermen are both impressed by the stove hurling out heat and decide to look into investing in one for their shack.

My tipi is the basic conical structure. Many tent users employ an additional porch that attaches to the door and forms a short tunnel entrance. This prevents the door of the tent from letting in rain. The entrance to my tent is a little damp this morning and I can see why such a porch would be useful. They are not a cheap addition so I decide that I'll get one next year as a treat. After an hour or so, the canvas of my tent is dry. The problem is that the stove is very hot and I can't pack the stove away, or take down the tent, until it cools off. So I sit drinking tea and waiting.

There are a few midges about, but it is late in the season for them now and they are nothing like the pestilential hordes that attempted to devour me in Glen Affric. Even though the tent door is wide open, I am pleased to see that the midges will not enter my refuge while the stove is still producing heat. That little piece of information is very welcome as anything that will keep me safe from their irritating jaws is valuable knowledge.

At last the stove cools down and I can begin to take down the tent. Experienced Highland campers will know what happens next. Before I can get the tent down, the rain returns. My tent is soon soaked again, so I'll need to dry it out when I get home. That's Highland camping. Getting home with a dry tent is a rarity.

Chapter 11
Letting the Old Man in

Since Covid-19 arrived, planning anything has become a lottery with it almost impossible to predict what will be allowed to happen a few months hence. In 2021 restrictions begin to ease and I form a plan to get half a dozen of my friends together at Inver hut in September. It starts, as these things often do, with a casual conversation I had with my friend Derek. Derek lives in Norwich and he and I have kept in regular touch throughout the pandemic via video calls. Sometimes, when the Covid-19 restrictions were at their height, he was the only person I would talk to for several days. Our regular video calls help both of us cope with the isolation.

Derek is an avid traveller, having been to many exotic destinations such as Peru, Vietnam and Cambodia. During the pandemic the farthest he has been able to go has been his allotment, where he passes the time by growing gigantic marrows.

"Why don't you come up to the Highlands?" I ask him during one of our video calls. "You'd enjoy it. We could go to a mountain hut."

Derek looks at me suspiciously from the far side of the video screen in his front room in Norwich. "But it's Scotland. It'll be cold and wet."

I can't deny that. "We don't have to go anywhere. We could sit by the fire, eat sausages and drink beer."

Derek's mind begins processing this information. "When can I come?"

That's where it starts –a simple plan for Derek and I to meet up. I'm not sure how but a week or so later the idea of meeting up has spread, a bit like a virus, to our mutual friends.

Joe will be coming up from his home near Girvan, a small town on the west coast of the Scottish Borders. Chris will tear himself away from his telescope and fly up from Bristol. Martin will take the train from Blackpool. Our old friend Phil is coming up from the Wirral and, of course, Derek will drive the 500 miles from Norfolk.

Our planning takes place in April. Pretty much all of it is against the current restrictions. So if the restrictions remain in place by the time we reach September, our little gathering is off. It's a long shot at best.

As the weeks pass restrictions slowly ease and the possibility of us meeting up in the mountaineering hut near Achnasheen slowly becomes greater. As it draws nearer I begin to worry; there are a lot of things that could go wrong. All of us are now in our late sixties, a difficult age. At this stage in our lives we are going through a reverse adolescence. Just as in our teenage years when we developed into adult men, we are now transitioning into old men. It's not an easy journey.

Our minds tell us we can still do the things we could in our youth while the aches and pains in our bodies remind us forcibly that we can't.

Derek and I are chatting on one of our regular video calls. "We could go up a mountain," he suggests cheerfully.

Derek's mind is full of images of us striding uphill enjoying the fresh air and stunning views. My brain fills with images of sprained ankles, heart attacks and rescue helicopters.

"No we can't," I respond emphatically. "I'm not being responsible for a mountain rescue disaster. We'll stay in the hut and drink tea."

Derek is not to be dissuaded entirely. "We could go for walk at least."

I'm forced to concede. "Only a short one then."

Hopefully I'll be able to prevent a group of older gentlemen, most of whom never do anything more strenuous than walking the dog, from venturing into the death zone.

When he turned ninety, someone asked Clint Eastwood how he kept so active. "I get up every morning and I don't let the old man in."

I can hear the old man knocking on the door right now – I hope he doesn't have a key.

Clint is right: old age is an attitude of mind. Some of my contemporaries seem to embrace getting old with open arms. Some of them regard "moving with the times" as an abomination. Martin refuses to own a mobile phone and won't use a debit card; he uses cash and things called cheques.

I imagine he writes with a quill pen by candlelight. He is by no means alone in his rejection of the modern age.

In a vain attempt to prevent our little gathering from becoming an old fart's convention, I draw up a swear list.

THE OLD CODGER SWEAR BOX

Charges

- Young people today … £2
- In my day … £1
- These mobile phones … £2
- Do you remember when … £1
- What I can't understand … £1
- The trouble is these days … £1
- You can't get them like that anymore £1
- That Internet … £1
- I don't hold with it £25

September arrives and with it the easing of restrictions, so much so that our little gathering can take place without fear of contravening the guidelines. It looks like we'll all make it with one exception. Martin refuses to adapt his behaviour to the changes of time in any way and will not wear a face mask. In England, Martin can legitimately travel on the train without a mask and is perfectly at liberty to breathe the virus over anyone he likes. In Scotland, however, we are made of sterner stuff and the wearing of masks on public transport is mandatory.

As the train makes its way north and crosses the border, Martin expects that Nicola Sturgeon's Storm Troopers will board the train, deporting him back to England when he refuses to cover his face. My assurances that the rules are not enforced as stringently as this fall on deaf ears.

On the assumption that Martin will make it to Achnasheen I offer to meet him at the station and drive him the two miles to the hut. Ever independent, Martin assures me that I won't be required and that he and Phil, who is travelling with him, won't need a lift. He intends to walk down the railway line to where it passes a hundred yards from the hut. That is illegal but I don't bother to point that out; Martin has obviously made his mind up and is convinced that is what they'll do. I'm equally convinced that they won't be walking those two miles and that I'll collect them from the station. I don't tell Martin this either, deciding that actions speak louder than words and I'll simply turn up. One thing is certain: Phil, a retired civil servant, is very sensibly risk-averse and when the moment arrives he won't walk down the railway.

A week later Derek and I are standing on the single platform of Achnasheen station watching the yellow-fronted diesel train approach. Derek, who has been a stalwart of the Legalise Cannabis campaign for over forty years, has a little more hair than me and flaunts it by putting it in a ponytail. We have a point to make so I'm wearing three face masks and he is wearing four. The train arrives and both our guests disembark, Martin having avoided the mask police. The idea of walking to the hut evaporates like a spilled cup of railway tea and we all drive to the hut.

That evening I pitch my hot tent a few yards from the hut. These days I prefer to sleep under canvas rather than indoors.

Martin, who is still a keen camper, inspects the tent. "This looks pretty indestructible. I wonder how long it will last."

This is an interesting question coming from Martin. He is a destroyer of gear and has the ability to break almost anything. He once bought a Karrimor rucksack which the manufacturers had rather rashly given a lifetime guarantee. Martin broke it so many times the manufacturers were endlessly repairing it. His rucksack may have played a significant part in the company eventually going bankrupt. To be fair, Martin is tall with aquiline features, and I suspect he is of Viking ancestry. I doubt if Vikings were ever very careful with outdoor gear.

The longevity of tents is something that is only recently becoming significant. The priority of manufacturers has long been to make their tents and cagoules as light as possible. The quest to save weight has meant that most tents won't withstand more than a few years of heavy use. The Tentipi gives very little concession to weight and certainly isn't a backpacking tent. Its sturdy construction does mean that it will provide many years of service with minimal maintenance.

This also means that its impact on the environment is minimal, with a very small carbon footprint. This is in marked contrast to the motorhomes that have become so popular in recent years, on average putting around twenty tons of carbon dioxide into the atmosphere. The manufacture of a canvas tent only generates a few kilograms yet, in my view, the tent allows much the same lifestyle as the motorhome, apart from the use of a shower and toilet.

When I began to explore the outdoors I never gave a thought to the environmental impact of myself or my gear. Years later, I learnt that the outdoor clothing I bought in the 70s and 80s had been leaching chemicals into the environment for years. All those dripping cagoules from thousands of walkers along the Pennine Way have left a chemical trail along the entire 270 miles. Manufacturers are now moving away from the ultra-lightweight towards equipment that has three or four times the lifespan and a much lower impact on our environment. Such equipment is likely to be heavier and more costly to buy initially, although if you average out the cost of these more durable garments over their lifespan the overall cost is likely to be around the same.

I examine the heavyweight canvas. "I expect I'll get twenty years out of this."

Even Martin might struggle to demolish a Tentipi.

Our weekend passed without incident although I think there were a few occasions when one or two of us, including me, may have had to contribute to the Old Codger swear box. Beer and sausages were consumed and worlds were put to rights beside the hut fire. No ankles were sprained or hearts attacked. So successful was our little trip that everyone present wanted to come back next year. I think we may have started a tradition.

Much to Mr Eastwood's relief, I never let the old man in.

Chapter 12
Glencoul

It's dark, I'm miles from anywhere in one of the most remote glens in the Highlands, Glencoul, and the bothy is nowhere to be seen. It's late October and winter is knocking at the door. The darkness is profound. The only light in this place is from my head torch, picking out the gouts of rain and sleet that swirl in from the heavens. I'm dripping wet from having had to wade through the dark waters of the river. As the cold water buffets against my thighs and seeps into the inner sanctum of my underpants, I search with my torch for a place I can climb up the bank. The far bank is defended by a wall of overhanging peat and I can't find a place low enough to climb.

"What the hell am I doing here?" I mutter to myself. I am an old man standing in a river in the middle of the night, miles from anywhere. This is insanity.

At last the bank dips and I fancy I might be able to climb up, but when I try the peat gives way and I fall back into the river. I try again. This time I manage to grab the grass on the lip of the bank, and am almost over it before the grass tears away and I am deposited into the water once more. The problem is the weight of my rucksack. I unbuckle it and prepare to hurl it up the bank in front of me. As I get ready to throw it, I have a vision of it bouncing off the peat, leaping back into the water and being carried away by the current. The thought of my food, warm clothes and whisky being carried out to sea sends a shiver down my already shivering spine. I take a deep breath and hurl my rucksack over the lip of the bank. It vanishes into the darkness.

Bothies have officially been open for a couple of months but, surprisingly for a bothy-lover like myself, I've not felt the urge to visit one until today. That's in part because I am enjoying life in my hot tent so much that I don't feel the need to go to bothies. The other reason is that those of us who are part of the bothy community had been expecting a deluge of visitors once restrictions were eased. With the pandemic far from over, I'm also uneasy about the prospect of sharing the intimate space of a bothy with a group of strangers. Recently the urge to return to these romantic shelters I love so much has returned and I can no longer resist.

The disappearance of my sack seems to imbue my tired legs with superhuman strength and in seconds I make an undignified but successful attempt to climb the bank. My rucksack is waiting for me just over the lip. Walking down the glen, water sloshing in my boots, I realise I have two possibilities ahead of me. Number one: I find the bothy, light the fire and spend a comfortable and cosy night there, warming my feet and congratulating myself on how clever I've been. Number two: fail to find the little shelter and spend a long, cold, wet night coming to terms with my own stupidity. The second option does not appeal, so finding the bothy will become the sole aim in life for the next hour or so of walking. Other considerations, such as earning enough to pay the mortgage or keeping my cholesterol down or writing my novel, are so far from my mind as to have ceased to concern me. Instantaneously my life has become incredibly simple. The things that seemed important only a few hours ago no longer have any relevance. Mountains can do that; it is one of their charms, that they have the power to distil the essence out of life. I have only one aim now which, put at its simplest, is to survive.

~

I am driving north from my home in Inverness and heading for Sutherland, perhaps the remotest corner of Scotland. I am later than I had intended. Somehow all those last-minute things you have to do, like stock up on gas, get some coal, and buy more food, have taken longer than I expected. I'd forgotten to buy dehydrated mashed potato, one of my hill staples, and so stop in the small fishing village of Ullapool to get a packet. The village, with its sea front houses and coach tour hotels, always feels like a frontier town. The roads heading here from the south are broad and modern but once they pass through the village, turning inland and heading north towards Elphin and Lochinver, they revert to the twisting narrow tracks they once were, weaving their way between remote lochs and hills. It's hardly surprising that the Vikings raided and settled here, given the village's obvious significance as a sheltered harbour. The name Ullapool betrays its Norse origins: it is derived from "Ulla-Bolstadr" meaning "Ulla's steading".

Heading out of the small supermarket with a tin of chicken in white sauce and dehydrated mashed potatoes, my go-to bothy meal, I notice that the wind has become colder. My jacket is speckled with rain as I climb back into the car. Here the locals dress in warm, practical jackets and are already armoured against advancing winter with woolly hats and gloves - so different from their Invernessian counterparts, only just over an hour away, dressed in more fashionable clothes in the milder climate of the Highland's capital "city". What it must have been like here, over a thousand years ago, when longboats berthed where the CalMac ferry now rides at anchor. I doubt, to be honest, if things have changed that much. Ulla and his mates no probably made their way to the nearest hostelry with the same enthusiasm as the ferry passengers do today, although fortunately modern tourists usually leave their battle axes at home.

Beyond Ullapool, it is a different country. As I pass the few scattered houses that make up the township of Elphin, the hills begin to rise around me. These are tough, rugged hills which have been around for a while and have no intention of going anywhere. Their summits are armoured with bare rock interspersed with small pools and deep peat bogs, and their flanks are lined with terraces. There are no car parks at the foot of these hills, no signposts from the Right of Way Society reminding you to pack your sandwiches and wear clean underwear "just in case". This is a little-travelled world and once darkness comes it will be absolute. Snow dusts the summits as great clouds race across the sky, turning the light across the landscape a steely grey. You must watch the road now –if you take your eyes off it, it darts unexpectedly round a bend and leaves you heading for a ditch.

I park my car on a hairpin bend. As I shoulder my pack and head off across the wilderness, I know it'll be dark before I reach the bothy but I'm confident I'll be able to find it, even without the light. The map doesn't show a track heading for the bothy but that can't be right, can it? There must be a path; it is probably just too faint for the Ordnance Survey to pick it up, I reason. The bothy should be easy to find. It's that word "should" that niggles. It goes along with a collection of other words and phrases that have frequently been the precursors to disaster, words like "no problem", "easy", "a piece of cake", and "what could possibly go wrong?".

The track leads across some precarious stepping stones that cross the river just as it emerges from Loch na Gainmhich, a dark stretch of water about a half a mile in diameter. From there the path begins to climb and, as I gain height, the weather deteriorates. The clouds, earlier broken up, have coalesced into a continuous rolling mass. Every few minutes another veil of rain, sleet and hail sweeps across the open hillside and batters against the back of my pack.

An hour or so brings me to the watershed and I stand on the summit of the pass. Here I pause, undecided. Ahead of me is wild country. This late in the year, the northern days are short and the daylight is already beginning to loosen its grip. Then the clouds part and the landscape is unveiled before me, a vastness of hills and fjords stretching into a seeming infinity. The Stack of Glencoul, a stubby tower of rock, stands proud above the surrounding hills. I recognise the features I studied earlier on the map in the comfort of my centrally heated lounge. I am fascinated by maps –they fuel my imagination. The landscapes they reveal draw me in, showing me glimpses of places I have never seen. What would it be like, I wonder, to stand on that small bridge, to sit on the shore of that Highland loch, to wake in the morning and take in the view from that bothy? This map has brought me here, to this place. Behind me is an easy retreat to civilisation. With the weather breaking, perhaps turning back would be the wisest decision rather than heading into such uncertainty alone. Briefly the glen below me is illuminated by a shaft of sunlight. It feels so close and I have come so far that to turn back now would be a disappointment and a defeat. After all, it's all downhill from here. How hard can it be? (Add that phrase to those on the list at the end of the recent paragraph.) Another phrase passes through my mind: *Go for it.*

A couple of hours later, saturated from wading across the swollen river, I am stumbling through tussocks of wet peat in the darkness along the floor of Glencoul. The map was right: there is no path, and progress is painfully slow. Now and again my head torch beam picks out a pair of glowing yellow eyes. I am walking through the bedrooms of herds of red deer. They stare at me for a moment or two before heading off into the darkness. Sometimes I pass by where they were standing only seconds before, and they are so close I can smell their wet hide and feel the warmth of their breath.

I count my steps. 802, 803, 804. I could switch on the GPS on my phone and be guided by an illuminated dot on a map that would require no thought or skill to follow right to the door of the bothy, but I want to do this the old-fashioned way. I want to get it right using the hard-won skills I acquired through years of walking through these hills in mist and snow. This sort of navigation is a dark art, more magic than maths.

I'm close now, maybe less than half a mile, but I know from bitter experience that in the darkness it's easy to pass within twenty yards of a bothy and never see it. I'm hugging the coast here, and there are strands of seaweed amongst the long grass, so this is no longer the riverside but the edge of the sea. This, I calculate, is where I should be. Now and again, I cast my head torch beam up onto the hillside in case I am further on than I think and walk past the bothy. The little shelter is between me and the sea now, on a small promontory. If I miss it I should be able to double back and trap the place. There's that word again, "should". It's late, I'm cold and wet, and "should" is not a word I want to hear. I don't want to hear myself think that the bothy should be here. I want to hear myself say, "There's the bothy!"

805, 806, 807. The step counting helps. In such uneven

terrain I know it's wildly inaccurate but it does tell me one thing: I am not yet at the point where the path turns away from the sea and heads inland to the bothy. That's the point I don't want to miss. I dare not overshoot. Looking at the map, I notice that close to the bothy are two small hillocks with the path passing between them. These I dub the Boobs of Glencoul. I'm aiming to pass right between them, to walk down their cleavage.

I reach 1,000 steps. Now it's maybe a hundred yards or so to where the route I've planned should turn. My head torch beam picks out an old stone wall running seawards, the first sign of civilisation I've seen for hours. Walls, I decide, mean buildings, and buildings mean warmth and food. I head up towards an obvious break. I bear right and after a hundred yards the ground on either side of me begins to rise, and with it so do my spirits. This feels right –I must be in the cleavage. Suddenly, there's a Land Rover track and a few yards beyond that is the unmistakable outline of a building. I head for the bothy door.

Yards from the bothy a stag steps onto the track ahead of me and roars a challenge, his breath clouding in the light from my torch. I'm alone, he's bigger than me and he has pointy things on his head, but I'm too tired to worry now. I blunder on towards him. Surely he's bluffing; I know I am. It turns out I'm the better poker player and he vanishes into the darkness. There at last, bright in my head torch beam, is the white ellipse of the Mountain Bothies Association sign. I'm there, I've made it. Now I wonder why I was worried after all, and what could possibly have gone wrong.

I spend the night surrounded by dripping clothing beside the warm glow of the fire. I can hear the stags roaring in the rain-soaked glen as I sit sipping a well-earned whisky in splendid isolation. The bothy sits at the edge of the sea loch. In this starless night I can see the lights of Kylesku, a tiny hamlet, glittering on the far side of the sea loch, the first sign of other people on this planet I have encountered all day. My plan is to walk there in the morning and hitchhike back to my car. That way I'll have done a reverse hill climb, having descended to the bothy from the hills above. That's quite a rare thing to do and even better if I don't have to climb back up to my car. I am the only person for miles tonight and the bothy book reveals that only a handful of folk have passed this way in the last few weeks.

By morning my clothes are still soggy but thankfully the rain has ceased. My boots are still damp, but I have the luxury of dry socks to at least save me from the ordeal of having to put wet socks on. As I leave the bothy, great grey clouds race across the sky. The wind carries on it the scent of salt water from the sea loch only yards away. My planned route will take me past Glen Dubh bothy and then round the coast to the bridge at Kylesku. But first, I have a shallow river to cross.

On the far side of the river, I can see a sign. It's too far away to read and I am curious to see what it says. Sadly, my time of having dry feet is short lived. Only yards from the bothy, I am forced to wade the wide river, full of spate water from the rain last night. After about twenty yards of wading I emerge from the river with the familiar feeling of water sloshing about in my boots.

Now I can read the official looking sign: "Do not pass this notice if orange disc is displayed as deer culling is in progress and there is danger of fatal injury."

Hanging beside the notice is a small orange disc. I wonder how long ago that disc was hung there. It could have been several weeks ago or it could have been yesterday. Highland estates vary in the extent to which they welcome walkers. This sign could be a real warning of danger or simply a deterrent aimed at warding off walkers. There is no way of knowing. If I continue, there is a remote possibility of being picked off by a high velocity round.

I imagine a tweed-clad ghillie, smoking gun in hand, standing over my inanimate corpse, smoking gun in hand. "Ah well, he ignored the sign. What can you do?"

Sadly, I decide the only option is to turn around and climb back over the hill to where my car is parked. It'll be a long hard slog and my feet are already wet from crossing the river. I'm not a belligerent man by nature but I can't help wondering which half-wit decided to put the sign on the far side of the river. It would have been a very simple thing to have put the sign on the other side and avoid folk like me having to get needlessly soaked. As I wade back towards the bothy, my boots fill with cold water and my mind fills with dark thoughts.

After an hour's walking I am back in the steep-sided glen, not relishing yet another river crossing and the hard climb on the far side. Then I notice movement ahead of me. To my amazement, a figure is coming towards me. At first I think it must be a gamekeeper but then I realise whoever it is is moving fast and must be a walker.

The figure comes close enough for me to see that it is a man in his early forties. He is tall, lean and blond, and carries a big rucksack and a broad grin. He walks towards me, grinning with his hand outstretched. His impossibly white teeth are set in a tanned face.

"Hi, I'm Cotton Joe," he announces in a Midwestern American drawl as we shake hands.

It feels very strange to see another person in this remote place so late in the year. Sadly I don't have a nickname. "I'm John. I never expected to meet anyone here."

"Me neither," he says with a laugh. "I'm walking the Appalachian Trail."

As far as I can recall, the Appalachians are in the USA so a remote Scottish glen is off route to say the least.

He notices my puzzled expression. "I mean the IAT, man. International Appalachian Trail. I been though Ireland and come up all the way through Scotland. Ain't far now."

"I've not heard of it." The concept sounds bizarre.

He smiles indulgently. He's obviously had to explain this to lots of people. "The trail connects where the Appalachians used to be. Before the continents divided."

"Oh, I see." I don't really.

Cotton Joe shifts his pack, trying to get more comfortable. He looks like a man who has carried his pack a long way, for so long that it's almost part of him.

He kicks resentfully at the uneven ground beneath us. "This is hard going. No path."

The terrain here is tough, endless tussocky grass, with only the odd faint deer track for a traveller to follow. "Yes, it's slow. Any kind of a path would be good but there's nothing."

"You doing the Cape Wrath Trail?" he asks.

I have to admit that, embarrassingly, my excursion is far less ambitious. "No, I'm just visiting the bothy."

His face brightens. "Yeah, I'll maybe stay there tonight or possibly go on to Glen Dubh bothy."

I tell him about the sign but he appears unconcerned. He is, after all, an American and probably well used to the sound of gunfire. We shake hands and part, and I watch his pack slowly retreat off down the glen. I hope Cotton Joe makes it.

The climb out of the glen looks steep and uncompromising. Somewhere there is a path but it doesn't start until well above the floor of the glen. I'm glad I burnt all my coal last night but despite that, my pack still feel disconcertingly heavy. *At least it isn't raining*, I console myself, as I splash my way across the stream, climb up the peat bank and begin the ascent.

Ten minutes later the heavens open and almost immediately I can feel water tricking into my cagoule and down the cuffs of my sleeves. One of the disadvantages of walking poles is that rain can find its way in when you raise your arms to use the poles on a steep climb. I'm dreading the effort of hauling myself up the bracken-covered hillside. When I expect a climb to get tough, I have a mental routine. I accept that what I'm about to do will be hard and just focus on the next step. Thinking too much about what might be coming gets too much for me and drains my will. For that reason, I pretend that there is nothing above me and make each step count. The unknown is always worse than what faces you immediately.

By the time I haul myself up over the lip of the glen and on to the barren plateau above, the rain has become a cascade. The landscape here is primeval. High on the shoulder of the hill there is nothing to mark the hand of man. Across the glen, the stack of Glen Coul rises like a volcano smouldering in the rain-filled clouds. The small streams that cross this rolling area of land are swollen to bursting point after days of rain. A mile away, a great waterfall plunges off the cliff and even at this distance I can hear the roar of falling water.

"Don't get lost," I remind myself. Sometimes the path is distinct where it has cut into the soft peat. In other places it crosses bare rock and I have to be careful as it would be easy to lose the way. In weather this foul I don't want to be wandering about trying to relocate a lost route.

By the time I reach my waiting car I am soaked, so I'm forced to change into dry clothes at the roadside in the midst of the torrent. An hour later I am luxuriating in the oily heat of Ullapool chip shop, revelling in the smells of frying chips, tomato sauce and vinegar. Being warm and dry after hours in the rain gives me enormous joy. Only very rarely do I allow myself the sinful indulgence of fish and chips. At my age fried food is like Superman's kryptonite, a dangerous indulgence. I dip the first chip into the crimson sauce and savour the wicked indulgence, sensing my arteries furring up for the final time. I'm ecstatic as the warm glow of the potato and oil begin to revive me. I sit warm and content, watching the rain run in rivulets down the far side of the chip shop window. Cocooned inside, I wonder where Cotton Joe is. Perhaps he is still striding on through the storm towards the shelter of the next bothy or perhaps he is prostrate in the heather, the victim of a stalker's bullet.

Chapter 13

A Lesson from the Wind

It starts a long way off. Several miles away, high in the corries at the upper reaches of the river, the wind gathers its forces like an army preparing to charge. I hear it roaring down the glen towards me. Battalions of furious atmospheric warriors jostle with each other as they sweep down through the dark night towards my tent on the valley floor.

Bang.

The wind hits the walls of my tent, trying to push it sideways. The tent reels under the pressure but will not give way. The conical design of the Tentipi is the best shape to survive the onslaught. Like a boxer, it rolls with the punches. The wind can't get a purchase on the steep-sided tent; the pressure slides off the angled walls rather than forcing it over. I have driven the tent pegs well into the ground and no matter how hard the wind tries, it can't dislodge them.

The wind howls, the canvas flaps and the chimney of the tent rattles. Then the probing wind finds a weakness. It blasts in under the skirt and rips the pegs in the base of the tent out of the ground. My temporary home fills with wind like a wild beast has invaded it. I have to leap into action to secure the floor of the tent again. I realise now that the pegs I am using to hold down the skirt are too short. They are only four inches long and I am wild camped in an area of thick grass. The main pegs that secure the corners of the tent are long enough to penetrate the earth beneath the grass but these short pegs are unable to get enough purchase and won't hold in the strong wind.

Using the short pegs is mistake number one, but as the tent jostles in the wind I begin to realise that I have made a bigger mistake: the tent is in the wrong place. I'm on a learning curve with this hot tent and I realise now that finding the right place to pitch the tent in winter is going to mean a lot more than simply locating a flat area of ground with enough depth of soil to take the tent pegs. I'm going to have to find somewhere more sheltered from the wind for my future winter camps.

I camped at this spot in August. Then, I was besieged by all manner of biting insects and craved the slightest breeze to keep the midges at bay. Now the wind is an enemy, doing all it can to demolish my canvas home. Despite the wind's best efforts, the Tentipi is of rugged design and isn't even close to being blown down.

The stove keeps me warm, despite the wind dislodging the pegs holding the skirt of the tent. I am learning new skills. Camping in foul weather is a craft and at the moment I'm making novice mistakes such as camping in the open and not having long enough pegs. This is the only way to learn.

"It's not easy. You have to learn what to do," Gary had said when I first saw this type of tent in Gairloch. Now I know what he meant. I will need to look for campsites amongst trees if I am to cope with winter storms. My tent survived the storm but I could have saved it from much of the battering it took had I pitched it in a more sheltered location. I'll have to learn to adapt.

Since I last used the stove, I've made two important modifications to it. The first was very easy. I noticed that the stove door did not seal tightly enough and that even when the circular vent in the door was closed, too much air was getting into the stove, so it was burning too fiercely. The simple remedy was to fit fire rope around the opening of the door to give it a better seal. You can buy fire rope from most hardware stores. The rope came with a tube of adhesive and I glued a length around the door which made an efficient seal.

The next modification was not so easy. The advice I got from other hot tenters via Facebook, when I raised the issue of being cooked in my tent at night, was to fit a damper in the chimney. A damper is a metal disk fitted inside the chimney which rotates in order to control the airflow and allows you to manage how hot the fire burns. After searching the Internet, I found one in the size I needed on eBay. I ordered it and expected it to arrive within days. When it didn't come I checked my order and realised I'd ordered it from a small company based in Chicago, USA. It took three weeks to arrive and had been manufactured in India. The four-inch disk of cast iron had crossed the Atlantic twice before ending up in the chimney of my stove.

Fitting it was pretty straightforward. I don't have any kind of workshop or garage as I live in a flat so I called on my friend Gavin, who lives with his wife, Mary, in a white cottage on the shore of Loch Ness. Together we drilled a hole either side of the chimney and fiddled with the spindle of my Indian damper until it fitted snuggly across the chimney. I never thought sorting out my stove would be such an international effort.

As the wind rises in Sutherland, I am grateful for the damper. When I close it down the stove is controllable, even in this high wind. Without the damper I'd be sitting in a tent inches from a furnace, like the fireman on the footplate of a steam train hurtling through the night.

All night, the tent is buffeted by the wind. I sleep only fitfully, woken every few minutes by a fresh gust shaking the tent in its jaws. I can normally sleep though most things and the most savage bothy storm can't keep me from sound sleep, but the tent is different. I dream I am on a bucking sailing ship in the midst of dark, angry waters. The ship heaves and rolls as I cling to the mast. At any moment the boat is about to capsize and hurl me into the white-capped waves.

At last the dawn comes, and with it the wind eases. As I kneel beside the river to fill my kettle for a morning brew, I take the chance to watch the sky and try to guess what the weather will do. To the south the river tumbles into the glen through wide, empty hills. These hills are not tall enough to attract the attention of Munro baggers or serious hillwalkers so they are left largely unmolested. The wind has dropped and, as the water surges into my kettle I notice ominous grey clouds building above me. While the kettle heats up I check the weather forecast. The next two or three days are peppered with raindrops. Last night the wind should have been light – it wasn't. Light winds are forecast for the next three days. The word "showers" appears a lot and we already know that the weather here can interpret this word with a generous liberalism.

This far north, only a handful of miles from the ragged shore of our island, the weather is unpredictable. Storms can sweep in over the sea and collide with the rugged coast with incredible speed, making the place a meteorologist's nightmare. I know that the weather here can be incredibly deceptive. It rained early last night but the early morning wind has dried my tent, and it is such a bonus to be able to take it down dry. My small flat near the town centre of Inverness has many advantages but drying out my big tent means opening it out in a bedroom and turning it over several times a day until it dries. That's a chore I could do without.

A small bothy, not far away, is calling me. I take down the tent while it's dry, pack it into my car, and head for the shore of Loch Hope. It's almost two years since I visited this little-known bothy. It feels strange packing my rucksack for a bothy after such a long gap. These remote shelters have been part of my life for so long that having them removed was painful – but now I'm going back.

I've chosen this bothy carefully. It's not known to many

folk. It's not managed by the Mountain Bothies Association, and its whereabouts are only known to an elite group of ardent bothy-goers. Chances are, there will be no one else there, so I'll feel safe. I follow the unwritten code of bothy folk: I never give out the name of these secret places. These off-grid bothies are cherished and the fear is that if they become too well known, they will become too popular and could be in danger of being closed if landowners find the number of visitors becoming an nuisance. I'm not sure how realistic that fear is, but it is a real fear to this small community –so I hope you'll forgive me if I don't name where I am going.

In the age of the Internet, there are no really secret places. A few moments on Google or with an OS map would reveal my destination, but that is something you'll need to do for yourself. There are no cars parked where the path to the bothy leaves the road, so with luck I will be alone there. The path descends from the road and passes through a small area of forest before it emerges on the lochside. I walk about a hundred feet along the shingle of the loch shore until the little white cottage emerges from the greenery.

I have to duck my head to pass through the low door and enter the musty-smelling building. In minutes I feel as if I have never left this place. The smell of smoke and damp, the chill of the air, and the sense of peace all enter my bloodstream like a rush of some narcotic. I am back. I unpack my tins of food and my packet of pre-cooked rice. It's a routine I know well, although the rice is a recent innovation; for some reason it seems healthier than the ultra-convenient but incredibly synthetic powdered mashed potato I have carried to bothies for the last ten years.

I place my food in a plastic bag and hang it from a hook on the wall. That's my way of keeping it safe from the hungry mice that inevitably inhabit these remote places. Mice are agile and have an incredible ability to find their way into the most secret of hiding places when there is a chance of food. They are determined and ingenious but, last I heard, they can't fly. Anything suspended off the ground should be safe.

Mice have infested the homes of man ever since the first caveman rested a half-eaten bone on the floor of his shelter and awoke the next morning to find it devoured by tiny teeth. Look at old oil paintings from hundreds of years ago and you'll see bags hanging from walls. Until I began to visit bothies I had no idea what these suspended bags were for. Now I realise they are there to keep food safe from rampaging rodents. As I've said, mice can't fly –let's be grateful that bats don't steal sandwiches.

Only yards away from the door of the bothy, the waters of Loch Hope lap against the shingle of the shore. As at so many bothies, there is a sense here of being close to the passing of the years. This is an old place. People have lived here for thousands of years, much longer than this bothy has stood on this spot for. On the hill, looking down on the grey slate roof of the old cottage, there is a graveyard. Many of the headstones are tumbled down. Some are in the process of falling over and sit at odd angles. Most have been standing so long that the inscriptions they once bore have been eroded away by wind and rain. We seek immortality by carving our names in stone, the oldest thing we can imagine, yet we forget that stone is just a fleeting thing in the vastness of time.

Those whose graves stand above this old bothy once had lives and loves, hopes and desires, children and family, yet they have been forgotten as if their lives lasted only for an instant. Only a hundred yards from here are the remains of a hut circle and a chambered cairn, a reminder of lives yet more ancient.

I spend a while watching the clouds plume white over Ben Hope as the day cools and the light begins to fade. The breeze has dropped and the sky has turned grey. A raven flies low across the loch, a dark jagged shape against the billowing clouds. The thin northern light picks up the white horses on the loch. Across the water, autumn has painted the hills with shades of rust, ochre and gold.

That night, as I watch the embers of my small fire flickering, the bothy weaves its magic spell. I am back in the world I had missed for so long. I have a peace and a sense of belonging I have long missed.

Chapter 14
Glen Affric

"This is steeper than I thought," I remark to myself as I haul my cart down to the lochside campsite.

The cart, loaded with my tent and stove, wobbles a little as I begin the descent, its wheels bumping over tree roots. From above, this had looked like a gentle slope but the further down I go the steeper it becomes. In another couple of steps the physics of this manoeuvre change dramatically. I am no longer hauling the cart –it is pushing me. I manage to hold it for a few seconds then I start to slide and the cart takes this as an opportunity to push me even faster. My boots scrabble for purchase but the slope is muddy and I just skid.

I'm gathering momentum, unable to stop. Gravity is no respecter of ageing mountain authors and any dignity I once had is long gone. In desperation I grab the trunk of a small tree and try to hold the cart. Realising that I have lost the fight, I try to turn the cart sideways to prevent it hurtling to destruction. At this point the cart decides to turn a somersault and hurl both the stove and me into the air. That's how I end up upside down in the heather, with the wind knocked out of me, cursing gently. The cart has escaped and gone back to the wild, and my possessions litter the hillside.

I mutter a few well-chosen oaths and stagger to my feet, rubbing my bruises. I've just learnt another valuable lesson. I now know that there is an angle of ground beyond which it is impossible to steer a garden cart. This is a useful lesson to learn –I just wish learning it hadn't been so painful.

With any pretence at dignity gone, I am forced to concede victory to the cart and carry the stove down the slope. This is still no mean feat as there prove to be numerous tree roots and sections of slippery peat trying to trip me up. After an ankle-twisting struggle I am able to carry the stove down the slope and place it on the small strip of sand. Then I have to return to where the cart upended itself to collect the tent and the rest of my belongings that lie scattered across the slope.

Just as darkness falls, I relax in the tent and light the stove. The campsite is perfect this evening. The wind drops to nothing. I am perched on a narrow finger of land between the hillside and two islands, no bigger than the average back garden. Here the glen is bursting with forest and the night drops silently around me.

This is not the campsite I had expected to use. On a summer hillwalking expedition I had spotted a short track leading down to a clearing by the lochside and thought it would make an ideal autumn campsite. When I arrived in the glen this afternoon, I went straight to that spot.

It was sheltered, flat and easily accessible for me and my

cart, but somehow it didn't feel like the right place to be.

In exploring wild campsites, I've come to realise that certain campsites feel right and others simply don't. It has nothing to do with geography or any rational process. It is to do with the heart of the place. The place will be your home, even if it is only for one night. If you are not comfortable there, do not linger. When we camp we do so for the contentment it brings us in being somewhere different, and for the feeling of connection to the environment around us. All my adult life I lived in flats and houses and worked in offices. All of these places were simply places of convenience. They were in areas I felt no connection with. I had not grown up there. My parents have not lived there. Each house or flat had rooms that could easily have been in another street, town, or perhaps even in another country. This is something that would have been inconceivable only a few hundred years ago. Centuries ago most people did not move very far. It's certainly true that there have always been people who moved long distances, like merchants and soldiers, and that there have been great migrations of people. Most folk, however, remained living within a small area or moved only very slowly until a few hundred years ago. They had a connection with where they lived that the industrial revolution severed. When we camp we are making a positive choice to go somewhere that we can connect to. It is one of the few times in our lives that we choose to stay somewhere because of the joy it brings us.

The backpacker may not have this luxury and be forced to

camp in the only place they can find once their weary legs refuse to carry them further. Even the through-hiker is making a positive choice to spend a series of nights in a landscape they love. Surely no one would choose to hike for days or weeks through a landscape they did not feel a connection to. This is the true joy of camping: to be able to stay somewhere simply because we like the place and it makes us feel good. I have learnt not to stay somewhere if it does not speak to me.

This place, embraced by the forest, sitting between the shore and two tiny islands, feels exactly right. In the darkness I can see little outside the walls of my shelter. The mid-phase Moon peeps weakly through the thick cloud like a white-faced ghost peering in through the curtains. The hills sink back into dark silhouettes. Every now and again the still surface of the loch catches the moonlight and flickers in the darkness.

Sitting inside my tent I cannot see where I am, but I can feel it. In this glen of immense forest there is not another human being for five miles. The sense of isolation is luxurious.

I love my flat in Inverness. It is central and convenient, and I am blessed with a view over the river. The downside is that it is in a town centre and sits between two of the main bridges that allow traffic to pass through the city. This means that every ambulance, fire engine and police car on their way to a call with sirens blazing passes within earshot of my flat. It is never truly quiet.

All that reaches my ears here on a night like this is the

water of the loch lapping against the shore and the belly of the stove rumbling as it digests another log. The great flexibility of camping is that, in these remote Highlands, I am free to site my tent and make my temporary home anywhere I like. That's the law. Perhaps in the busy summer months, were I to camp in some of the hotspots like the North Coast 500 or in Glen Coe, I might attract attention. In the empty months of winter no one cares where I camp. Passing locals who notice my tipi will no doubt shake their heads and wonder at the lunacy of anyone willing to camp in these months of darkness and cold.

The next morning I wake in Glen Affric, a few miles away from my midge-besieged lightweight camp. This long valley is a gem of the Highlands at any time of year, but in autumn it blooms into colour as the trees of the forest turn vivid shades of gold and ochre and a hundred shades of brown. I know this glen well and have walked here many times, but it is so vast a place that you could come here over and over again and never have to repeat the same route. Last night the air was still and the only sound all night was from the waters of the loch lapping at the shore. Today I can see ominous grey clouds gathering over the hills to the west. They are the portent of wilder weather to come. I wonder if I can risk a walk around Loch Affric, a route I have never completed in full. I have wandered beside this loch many times. I've camped on its shore and backpacked along the south side of the loch to reach the remote Camban bothy. I must have climbed every hill on both sides of the glen, some several times. Despite all these trips there is an undistilled magic in this place that draws me to it again and again.

The route starts from the car park at the end of the loch, a couple of miles away. Stepping out of my car, memories of the last time I was here come flooding back. I recall vividly July of last year when, having been released from lockdown, the urge to escape into the hills was overwhelming. I came here and was even glad to spend a night besieged by midges if it meant I could be in the hills once more. The last time I was in this car park I had hurled my rucksack into the car, frantically trying to rid myself of the scourge of thousands of tiny hungry jaws. On my last trip I had fled this place, rather than simply left.

Today is very different. The glen is empty of people and, much to my relief, there are no midges either. The car park's picnic tables are vacant and a sign on the toilet block says they are closed for the winter as it would be impossible to prevent them freezing solid at this time of year. The sign goes on to give the helpful information that there are toilets available at the Dog Falls car park. They are composting toilets that don't require water. Anyone driving here would have passed Dog Falls over twenty minutes ago. Let's hope no one reading this sign is in a hurry.

I take the path down the eastern side of the loch. It begins as a wide Land Rover track but very quickly becomes a narrow but well-made path. Below me is the head of the loch, with Affric Lodge and its outbuildings sitting on a series of small islands. I have mixed feelings about such lodges. There are thousands across the Highlands. They were built by Victorian landowners as ostentatious displays of wealth, symbols of sporting estates where the destruction, rather than preservation, of wildlife was seen to be of paramount importance. Most are fake castles with turrets and battlements, reflecting Queen Victoria's love of a mythical Highland way of life and Prince Albert's passion for hunting.

Affric Lodge is no different. I glimpse its turrets through the trees across the loch. Despite my distaste of the buildings as symbols of oppression, I can't deny that the handful of white cottages and outbuildings sitting on islands in the waters of this magnificent loch is one of the most evocative sights in the whole of the Highlands. My imagination never ceases to be fired up by such places. Dwelling in a place like this must be an inspiring experience. Many of these lodges are no longer lived in and their maintenance is a drain on any estate, yet the images they create of a romantic Highlands are a credit to the Victorian imagination. I defy even the most cynical of hillwalkers not to be stirred by the sight of Affric Lodge.

Beyond the lodge the path climbs gradually and to my right the hills rise steeply. One night, many years ago, not long after I first moved north and joined the local mountaineering club, I met Ray at one of the club's regular Thursday pub nights. Ray had moved north from his native Luton a few years before me. He looked every inch the mountaineer with his blond curly hair, rugged complexion and wild beard. All mountain men wore beards in those days;

it was a legal requirement. Ray bought me several pints of heavy and began talking enthusiastically about climbing the hills above Loch Affric. Ray was on his way to completing all the Munros and there was one particular remote hill he was desperate to climb, but he didn't have a car at the time so needed to get someone else interested in the exploit. As I sipped the third beer he had provided, he casually asked if might want to come with him on the walk. Mellowed with alcohol I agreed instantly, not realising that he'd been trying to persuade other club members for weeks without success.

When I picked Ray up in my old Marina estate the following Sunday morning, I had no idea what I'd let myself in for. Ray set off along the very path that I am walking today and just kept walking. I expected him to set off up each hill we came to, but he just walked on and on. I was used to walking in the Lake District where you drove to the foot of the hill and climbed it from there. Having to walk for several miles even before we could start climbing came as a shock to both me and my legs. I was already tired by the time Ray at last headed up towards the summit of one of the hills, cheerfully explaining to me as we went that we might be able to see the hill he wanted to climb from the summit of this one. We made it back to Inverness ten minutes before closing time in the local pub and managed two pints before we were thrown out. I learnt to be cautious of Lutonians bearing beer after that.

That was one July many years ago. This is November and a very different day from that sunny July Sunday in 1978 when the sky was a peerless blue. Today ominous clouds are building from the west, threatening to soak me at any moment. As the far end of the loch approaches, the landscape takes on a wilder aspect. This is a remote spot. I've walked six miles from the roadhead and the only way to return is on foot. Crossing a small stream, I twist my ankle painfully and am reminded that I sprained it only a few weeks ago.

I realise I need to be careful where I step. I've walked quite a long way by now and hobbling back to my car on one foot would be very difficult. After a while the pain eases, but this is the farthest I have walked on the ankle since the injury, and I realise now that it isn't fully healed.

I have a strategy in dealing with injuries, that I've developed over the years. Many years ago I suffered crippling back pain that left me barely able to walk at all. Trips to the osteopath brought little relief. Eventually I persuaded my doctor to refer me to a physiotherapist. She told me to concentrate on exercising my core muscles, a set of muscles I'd never heard of.

I began exercises in the gym to strengthen my core. It wasn't easy and it took about two years to fully overcome my back problem. At first I was barely able to walk two hundred yards, but it gradually improved. As my spine straightened out I got slightly taller and my back pain slowly went away. Today I have virtually no problem with my back at all. I still exercise it and now I can lift heavier weights in the gym than I ever could. At sixty-six I am stronger than I was at thirty-six.

That experience has taught me a valuable lesson: whenever

I get any injury I work on it intensively. The Internet, especially YouTube, is a fantastic resource. My ankles have been prone to injury for years, as have my knees. As any hillwalker knows, your knees are your Achilles heel –if it's possible to have a heel in your knee, that is. I know that if you use exercise and rest in the right way, in time you can overcome many injuries. Two weeks ago I had my ankle elevated and under pressure from a cold compress. Over about a week the swelling went down and I began to slowly stretch and strengthen my ankle.

Now I am walking around this remote loch, wondering how sensible this is when I know my ankle isn't as stable as it should be. I reach the far end of the loch around mid-afternoon. Where the loch ends, the glen broadens briefly before it leads on west to where Glen Affric Youth Hostel sits in the valley floor. Further west still, the glen narrows once more to a steep-sided V-shape, with Camban bothy a few miles further down. As it's November the hostel will be closed now, although the existence of the Affric Way will probably ensure that the bothy gets a steady trickle of visitors. Good news for the resident mice. Although the hostel is closed, the YHA leaves one room open and accessible as an emergency shelter. It has no fireplace and is furnished only by a handful of bunks with no mattresses. Basic though it is, that shelter would prove a lifesaver if you were caught out by a storm in this remote place.

I've been walking for three hours and my legs are beginning to remember just how old I am when I arrive at the romantically named Strawberry Cottage. This is a mountaineering hut, available for clubs to rent, that gives access to the hills here. It sits just above the main river that flows into Loch Affric. One stormy winter's day I was really grateful for the hut when I was returning from Camban bothy in heavy snow, and by the time I reached Strawberry Cottage the snow had turned to sleet and I was wet and chilled to the bone. Although the cottage was locked, the porch door was open and I was grateful to take shelter in it as the wind and sleet battered against the door. There were two water containers in the porch and I made use of one of them to get my stove out and cook some soup. I was very grateful of the warming soup as it brought the sensation back into my fingers and heated my core. As I enjoyed the last of the soup I read one of the notices in the porch. It informed me that the two water containers were not drinking water but were there to flush the cottage's outside toilet. There are some things it's better not to know.

Today, although the clouds are looking increasingly ominous, I am happy to say they seem to be moving very slowly and I'm hoping to outrun them before they can disgorge their contents onto me. Great rolling masses of dark clouds crash into the hills above me, their outlines picked out by the low sun. The track on the south side of the loch is a broad Land Rover track and is well maintained by the estate. Although it climbs up and away from the waters of the loch, it is easy going and I make good time over the last three or four miles to the car park.

When I'm about a mile from the car park, I realise the daylight of this winter day is almost done. Darkness creeps in from the hills around me and the trees of the forest turn to silhouettes. It's now that I stumble over a stone I couldn't see in the darkness and my ankle shoots pain into my calf. I stagger and almost fall, crying out with pain and then resort to yelling curses in the empty glen. Luckily I find I can walk, even if it is with a limp now. I hobble the last half-mile and reach the car just as night closes in. My ankle is throbbing but it has held up, so all the work I have been putting in has clearly helped. As I drive back down the glen with the weight off my ankle, the pain eases. I've done no permanent damage to it.

My campsite is silent and dark. My head torch picks out the conical outline of my tent and the reflective guy lines show its position amongst the deep darkness of the forest. It is a degree or two above freezing on this November night. The tent feels cold and damp, having been empty for all the hours I have been walking. My legs are tired and I sit shivering for a few minutes, lighting the paraffin lamp and loading kindling and wood into the stove from my chair. I love the gentle light of the paraffin lamp. I'm a sucker for these lamps. I bought this one and spent hours polishing its brass body so that it gleams. Polishing brass is a pointless task as it will slowly tarnish and I'll have to polish it again, but it's something I find relaxing and oddly rewarding.

It's now that the hot tent shows its worth. One match and the stove springs into life, yellow flames dancing in its belly.

I'm always surprised by how quickly the hot tent warms up. Within five minutes of lighting the stove, the tent is warm and I can enjoy the heat of the stove, feeling the muscles in my legs warm up and relax. I cook my meal over the wood-burning stove and enjoy a dram or two in the warmth and comfort only possible in a hot tent.

I like to visualise the scene outside my tent. This great glen is empty now, the darkness unbroken for miles around me. There are no streetlamps, not even a single light from a cottage window, to disturb the blanket of dark. The only sounds are the wind sighing through the forest and the loch lapping against the shore.

If you could look down on this scene, you would catch the occasional glimpse of the moon breaking through the clouds and casting its reflection on the water of the lake. The only other light in the blackness would be my tent, the light from the paraffin lamp making it glow orange in the sea of black. Perhaps the smoke from my stove might catch in the moonlight now and again. A rare thing this, to be able to experience such solitude on this hectic island. To me it feels an enormous privilege to have this vast space to myself. It would be nice enough to be here in a lightweight tent. In such a tent I would need to be in my sleeping bag by now to ward off the cold. There is a pleasure in that, but the hot tent feels like a luxurious palace compared to the confines of my backpacking tent. It's such a contrast to the last time I slept in this glen, in the summer when I lay trapped in my two-man tent. I was alone then and enjoying the solitude of my return to the hills –if you don't count the two million midges waiting outside the entrance of my tent –but the hot tent feels like a different world, more like a home than a temporary shelter.

The tent has opened opportunities for me that I didn't anticipate. I realise now that my fondness for winter bothy visits had limited what I did in the hills. It's odd how you can fall into habits without realising it. Visiting a Highland bothy in the winter, especially in December when the nights are so long, means that you have to carry in quite a bit of fuel if you don't want to spend the night shivering. This means a heavy pack, especially if, like me, you prefer to travel alone. This makes it difficult to spend more than one night in the bothy; so doing any exploration beyond the bothy is difficult as you have to walk out the following day. Winter days are short so options are limited. By using this tent I am able to go for reasonable walks and return to what is, I suppose, my base camp. Not only have I somewhere warm but, if I get soaked, I can also dry out my clothing –a really important consideration if I am spending a few nights out.

Gavin asked me if I could send him a photo of the stove in action. Happy to oblige, I set the camera up and took a picture of the stove with the damper handle featured. When I looked at the image, all that was visible was the stove and there was no way you could tell that there was even a fire in it. The solution was obvious: open the door. If you'd asked me before if I could take a picture while lunging backward to escape flames belching ferociously from the stove door I'd have been pretty doubtful if I could manage it. It turns out I did a reasonable job of the photo and of saving both myself and the tent as the flames leapt from the open door. My mistake had been to leave the damper closed when I opened the door.

This was the first time I had opened the stove door with the damper in the chimney closed. Until this night, I hadn't even possessed a damper I could close. If you open the door and the chimney is open and undamped, the flames are sucked harmlessly back into the stove. I now know that if the damper is closed the fire leaps out from the front of the stove like a demon escaping from the gates of hell. I realise that I still have a great deal to learn in my hot tent journey. I had thought that I knew all I needed to know about camping but fire-breathing stoves, relentless winds and wayward carts have revealed to me that I have a great deal to learn.

Chapter 15
Brigadoon Post Office

Every now and again something occurs which makes me think, "That could only happen in the Highlands", like when the police helped me to steal petrol or when, one Hogmanay, a garage owner handed me the keys and said, "Help yourself."

It's the remoteness of the Highlands that makes it unique. I was arranging my car insurance not long ago and the telehandler assured me that no one was ever more than ten miles from a garage. I didn't even try to correct her. The islands are even more isolated, and sometimes the inhabitants of such places have to find solutions to problems that just would never occur to folk in the more populous areas of our island.

I find myself experiencing something like this in December when I head over to Inver hut at Achnasheen for a few nights. A reader called Nathan has asked me to post a copy of *Wild Winter* to his father, Kelvin, for Christmas. Kelvin has enjoyed my earlier books and Nathan wants to get him my latest book. I don't normally send books to readers directly –that's what publishers are for –but Kelvin has spent over thirty years working in mountain rescue on Dartmoor. I really can't let someone down when they had made such an important contribution to the safety of others. I have the book wrapped up, but posting it in time for Christmas, only a few days away, proves a challenge. I am in a hurry to get to Achnasheen as the weather is deteriorating and the wind is starting to pick up in Inverness. Over on the west coast, in the exposed glen where the Jacobites Mountaineering Club's hut resides, it will be much rougher. The hut is surrounded by deep bog which is prone to flooding so the club have constructed an extensive wooden walkway which is sometimes as high as four feet above the bog. This raised walkway is not for the fainthearted in a high wind so I want to get there as quickly as I can.

In the end I have to abandon posting my book for Christmas and head west. I hate letting anyone down and feel guilty for not getting the book in the post. I call in at the village shop in Contin on the off chance that they might have a post office, but no luck. I resign myself to the fact that I'll have to post the book in a few days once I get back from Achnasheen. It will probably be too late for Christmas. As I drive west along the broad sweeping road that heads over to Achnasheen, the clouds grow increasingly menacing and the trees beside the road wave more and more as the wind picks up.

The village of Achnasheen is little more than a halt on the railway line between Kyle of Lochalsh and Inverness. There is an unmanned station, a dozen or so houses, and a one-room café which sprang up a couple of years ago when the route of the North Coast 500 was established, running past the small community. In Highland terms you would class the place as a village, although in the rest of Britain it probably wouldn't register as anything more than a road junction. This is the last sheltered place before the parking for the mountaineering hut, so I pull in here to avoid having to get ready in the middle of a howling gale. I put on my cagoule and snow gaiters, armouring myself for the short but exposed walk into Inver hut.

I'm just about to drive away when I notice something odd –the lights are on in the station. I'm sat wondering why that could be when a woman walks past the car window, carrying a package, and goes into the station. It's then that I spot a sign for the post office with some faded text beneath. When I get out of the car and read the text, it tells me that there is a post office in the station that exists once a week on a Tuesday between 2:00 p.m. and 4:30 p.m. I check the day –it's Tuesday. I look at the time –3:55 p.m. The post office should be open.

Sure enough, to my astonishment, an older woman sits at a desk in the brightly lit station with stamps spread out in front of her. The woman with the package is watching while the woman behind the desk goes through the mysterious ritual that post offices always follow. She tries to squeeze the package through a variety of oddly shaped holes and then begins to discuss which of the many thousands of tariffs will apply to get the package to its destination. I wait patiently with my books. Obviously I have to queue –well, it is a post office. I'm astounded by the synchronicity of it. It's as if this post office materialised out of thin air just so I can post my book. After I leave, maybe it will dissolve into the mist and there will be nothing to show that it ever existed.

In another startling piece of luck, the wind drops to virtually nothing when I park my car at the start of the walkway to Inver hut. I sling on my rucksack and make a run for it. In the distance there is a rising howl. This is the next gust of wind rushing up the glen, about to hurl me from the bridge and into the swollen river waters. At this time of year there is a pervading greyness in the sky and the landscape. The river has burst its banks and the bog beneath the walkway has sunk beneath two feet of dark floodwater which swirls and eddies around the supports of the walkway. This is not a good place to get blown into the water carrying a heavy rucksack. I am relived to make it off the exposed walkway just as the wind arrives with malicious intent.

Inver is a cold place even in the best of weather, which this is not. That evening I have to burn twenty kilograms of coal on the lounge fire before the room is warm enough for me to remove my duvet jacket and enjoy a quiet evening watching the flames dancing in the hearth. My plan is to stay in the hut for a few days as nobody else is booked in until after Christmas. Inver is a good place to come when the nights are long and dark. At this time of year, I would be confined to my tent from around three thirty onwards. That's a long evening sat beside a stove. Inver has electric lights and the huge advantage that I can fill my car to the brim with food, coal and drink, so supplies are never an issue –provided the storm demon doesn't catch me on the walkway, that is.

Sadly my plans are overturned when I get a message from the hut custodian to tell me that someone has decided to book the hut for the next weekend. I'm there on a Tuesday night, and the current Covid-19 regulations mean that the hut has to be vacant for at least two nights between visitors. Before the pandemic I had used the hut fairly frequently mid-week, as most Jacobite members and other mountaineering clubs book the hut at weekends. As I'm retired, weekends have long since ceased to have any meaning for me. Although I would like to stay a few nights to enjoy the wild weather, I don't mind giving way to other folk. I always feel that when it comes to using the hut other folk should have priority. I have the luxury of time that most people, with the irksome burden of employment, don't have. I also have lots of other places to camp or bothies to visit, even if during December these places are a little less attractive than they are normally. I can also drive to the hut in under an hour from my Inverness base. Most Jacobite members have to travel for well over three hours, so I have it easy. The following day I pack up and head home.

By late December 2021, the scourge of Omicron is menacing the nation and none of us knows what the next few months will bring. This makes me doubly grateful to have squeezed in a visit to Inver as the prospect of further trips seems bleak. As I write this, chief clown Boris Johnson continues to ride his monocycle around the circus ring. The only thing that surprises me about this outlandish performance is that he has managed to stay in the saddle for so long. By now the audience is beginning to tire of his comedic dance. In the wings, I can hear the lion tamer getting his beasts ready for their entrance. They sound hungry and the clown looks nervous.

Chapter 16

The Bothy Butler

"Don't look down" is advice you'll often hear on the hills when you're in a scary high place.

As I get older, I find it a good idea not to look down to avoid glimpsing my slowly expanding waist. In an effort to halt this almost inevitable decline, I decide to follow the example of walking author, Alex Roddie. Alex and I have known each other for some years now. We first met virtually when I was writing my one-man play about mountaineer George Mallory. I was wavering in my determination to get the play written and it was Alex's encouragement over the UKClimbing forum that gave me the motivation to complete it.

Alex was working in a mobile phone shop where the long hours and the mind-blowing stupidity of many of his customers was taking its toll on his sanity. When we first began having discussions over the internet, he was about to try and set himself free from the technological nightmare of phone sales by becoming an editor for outdoor writers and a feature writer for magazines like *The Great Outdoors*. Alex later edited my first book, *The Last Hillwalker*.

I like working with Alex because he and I are so different. He is thirty years younger than I am and is able to detect any tendency I have to go into old fart mode, something I am prone to do on long winter evenings. Now that I'm in my late sixties I suddenly find phrases like "in my day" and "young people today", or even the dreaded, "now you see what I don't understand is …" popping unexpectedly out of my mouth. I try and guard against becoming an old codger but I have the feeling that, like old age and the urge to wear a cardigan, it will inevitably creep up on me.

We first met face to face in the remote Maol Budhie bothy when Alex was walking the Cape Wrath Trail. Alex is an expert in lightweight hiking. I carry enough supplies to ensure my comfort under any circumstances. Any fool can be uncomfortable in the hills; it takes skill and experience to travel the Scottish hills with a degree of luxury. Alex even refuses to wear boots, preferring lightweight walking shoes. Nor does he carry a stove, instead subsisting on concoctions he can eat cold. No stove! No tea in the morning to look forward to! What kind of camping is that? In my day …

When I met him for the first time, I knew he'd been existing on meagre rations for over a week. I played Jeeves to his Bertie Wooster and carried in spaghetti bolognese with chocolate cheesecake for dessert, and a rather nice red wine – just to show him how it should be done.

"May I recommend the red wine, sir?"

Alex happily accepted the red wine, which was good because it was the only wine. Sadly I can't carry in a cellar. He dined well that evening, thanks to his hiking butler.

We parted company in the morning, when Alex set off north having breakfasted on dried dog food.

Alex is now a lean, fit long-distance hiker who is perfectly at home strolling through the Alps for day after day. This isn't how he's always been. Stints as a barman in Glen Coe and the enforced inactivity of working in a mobile phone store had left him a little pudgy. His answer was to walk for an hour every day before breakfast. I decide I will give it a try, although rather than walking I will cycle. By December another lockdown in some shape or form seems inevitable. Perhaps my saviour will be my bike.

I have an on–off love affair with cycling. Over the years, I have had a pattern of cycling for several months and then completely quitting. This pattern has partly been enforced by the Highland weather. I cycle regularly during the summer, just about manage to get bike-fit, and then the winter arrives and the weather brings an end to activities. The cycling from my home in Inverness takes me into the hills above Loch Ness, and is often is spectacular.

Once you make the stiff climb out of the town and into the hills, that's about 400 feet of ascent. You can cycle for miles, past lochs and hills, on roads that are largely bereft of traffic. The problem I have experienced year after year is that once the temperature drops in winter, keeping even vaguely comfortable on a bike is very difficult. I arrive at the top of hills overheated, gasping and dripping sweat. Gasping for air and dripping sweat is my standard mode for cycling these days. The problem arises when you then have to freewheel back down the hill. On the way down through the frigid air, you slowly turn into an icicle and lose the use of your hands fairly quickly, not to mention that the cold air can do things to a gentleman's anatomy that I am reluctant to discuss.

My cycling has followed a predictable pattern over the last few years. I'd start off in the spring, unfit and gasping. I'd spend the summer slowly increasing my fitness and talking steeper and steeper hills, only to have to abandon cycling altogether as autumn arrived, bringing with it colder weather. I know that dedicated cyclists bolt their bikes to some sort of roller contraption and spend the winter months pedalling up cyber hills in the back bedroom. I don't have that level of dedication.

Things changed when I bought a mountain bike. To explain this, I need to rewind a little. I bought the cheapest mountain bike I could find about five years ago. My plan was to cycle into some bothies and to use the bike on Land Rover tracks to help me get to more remote hills. I had no intention of risking life and limb performing Lycra-clad gyrations on death-defying descents. Delusional though I am, I do know that I am at least forty years too old for that.

"Age is just a number," they say. Really? Try performing a back flip at the age of sixty-two. I think you'll find the "number" is the fractures they count while X-raying your vertebrae in casualty.

Shortly after I bought the bike, the bearings in the back wheel collapsed. It was a cheap bike, after all. To be fair to the bike, I had fitted panniers to it, loaded it up with coal and beer and then cycled in to Glen Beg bothy. I had cycled most of the way to the bothy, but then made the mistake of hauling the bike through a deep bog that covers the last mile of the route to the shelter. The poor bike groaned and creaked in pain on the return journey. I always meant to get it fixed but somehow never got round to it. I reverted to enjoying tarmac runs on my road bike, leaving the mountain bike languishing in the back of the shed for several years, neglected and unloved. When Covid-19 struck I decided that I should resurrect my mountain bike and make a determined attempt to use the machine again. I fiddled with the bike and got some mates to look at it, but the creak refused to go away. Eventually my local bike shop got it sorted and I was once more able to cycle about on it.

My revelation with the mountain bike came when I discovered a track that led along the side of the Caledonian canal. This track would have been beyond the capabilities of my road bike but the mountain bike handled it easily. As you'd expect, the canal route is devoid of hills so I could cycle along it without having to brave the icy cold winds of winter on any downhills. The mountain bike had another advantage: it was hard work. Road bikes are great but they are so easy to ride that you have to travel a long way to feel the benefit on your body. The mountain bike had my legs protesting after only a couple of miles. I had found a way of cycling through the year, rather than abandoning the wheels every winter and having to start over when the summer came.

Also, as Christmas approaches this year, I decide to avoid the gym in order to reduce my chances of contracting Covid-19 which would end my chances of seeing my daughters together for the first time in two years. The bike is the solution.

Alex's example of walking every morning before breakfast is impressive. I am not sure I'll be able to emulate that. I've never been able to exercise first thing in the morning. It normally takes me a few cups of tea before I am even able to muster the energy to stir my porridge. I decide that I will give it a try and see if it is something I can do. I also have to make another decision: what will I do about the weather? I realise that if I worry about whether it is too wet or too cold or too windy, I will waste lots of time vacillating. I have to make up my mind to go out on the bike no matter what the weather is. If I approach it in that way, there is no decision to make. Some mornings I might get wet or cold. Sometimes I might find the struggle against the wind too much, but since I only plan to cycle for thirty minutes every morning I will never be more than fifteen minutes from home. The odd soaking won't kill me. If I don't take this approach I'll spend every morning looking out of my window and not making my mind up until it's too late.

The first morning feels wrong; my body wants to sit drinking tea for an hour before even thinking about moving, but I go through the process. I put on my bad weather cycling gear, which is really a version of my average winter hill gear minus the boots. I climb on my bike and set off. It's nine in the morning and I've only had a cup of tea. It feels wrong but soon the rhythm of cycling takes over. I cycle along the riverside, then across the A82 which is the main road to Fort William. There are pedestrian lights here that slow me down, but at least they allow me to catch my breath before I cycle down the road beside the River Ness.

Fortunately these are quiet roads. For the most part, they are one-way and cycle-friendly. In the town centre, I pass the hotels that front the river. Normally they would be bustling with tourists but during these days of the pandemic there are only a handful of hotel guests loading their suitcases into taxis. Then I pass the city's cathedral, a red brick monolith. Beyond that sits the glass front of Eden Court theatre. There are posters outside for Cinderella, the first pantomime for two years. Life blood for the struggling theatre.

A few minutes more cycling and I'm passing by the first of the Victorian footbridges that cross the river, then I'm out into the playing fields and parklands at the edge of town. Inverness glories in the title of a city but it is really no more than a large town and I can cycle to its fringes in only fifteen minutes. In less than half an hour I am back at my flat putting my bike back into its shed. I feel exhilarated after the bike ride and enjoy my morning porridge with great enthusiasm. I don't know if cycling everyday will reduce my waistline but I am certain that it will raise my mood.

My morning cycles have become part of my routine. I find myself looking forward to them. After each ride, I return home invigorated. I wonder how long I'll keep it up for ...

Chapter 17

Torridon

I spend the last few days before Christmas watching weather fronts sweep in across the Atlantic. Around the shortest day the weather settles and I can see a chance to catch a couple of days camping before my daughters arrive for Christmas. My youngest daughter spent last Christmas confined to her care home by Covid-19 restrictions. My eldest daughter and I were able to visit her wearing masks, gowns and gloves. We couldn't hug her, and managed what Christmas we could by opening presents together and pulling socially distanced crackers. Now, with Christmas only a week away, we are all hoping that we can dodge the Omicron variant long enough to be able to have that time together. If the virus finds its way into her care home and they have to go into lockdown, or if any of us have to isolate, our second Christmas will be ruined. For that reason I am being ultra-careful so bothies are out as I can't risk meeting other folk in such confined spaces, but maybe I can snatch a couple of nights in the hot tent.

When the weather is dodgy I try to go somewhere

relatively local. I'm so lucky to live in the Highlands where there are some great places only an hour away. Even if I did have to drive seventy or eighty miles, it's nothing like the chore it is on the traffic-choked roads of southern England. In the winter even the main roads here are quiet. I decide to travel to Torridon, one of my favourite places. Even if the weather keeps me off the higher peaks, I'll have a chance to explore the margins of Loch Maree and the woodland there, one of the last remnants of the old Caledonian forest. I never lose my fascination for these ancient woodlands.

I arrive at Taagan campsite near the tiny Highland village of Kinlochewe. As I expected it is deserted, and would be the perfect place to camp if it were not for one thing –the laminated sign pinned to the campsite notice declaring the place closed. I have a history with this place. I recently began to enjoy the grumpy old man's favourite pastime: complaining. Around this time last year I came to this campsite and found the same sign. As the campsite is part of the Bienne Eighe Nature Reserve, I contacted NatureScot, which used to be called Scottish Natural Heritage (SNH). Why the organisation changed its name from SNH to NatureScot, I have no idea. I thought the old name was fine. It told you what the organisation was about. NatureScot isn't even grammatical.

NatureScot got back to me and told me that, contrary to the message clearly printed on the makeshift sign, the campsite was open. They explained that the small basic toilet block was closed but that I was welcome to camp there and use the visitor centre facilities about half a mile away. That was good news to me. The campsite is ideal for winter camping. It is restricted to tents only, so there will be no campervans or caravans. Perfect for me and my hot tent. In the winter it is rarely used by other folk so you can have the place to yourself. Whilst I wouldn't describe the site as scenic, there are some great walks within easy reach and it makes a great winter base. In the summer I avoid the place like the plague because it is midge-central and if there is no wind, anyone foolish enough to camp there will get eaten alive. The campsite is free but in the midge season you'd have to pay me to camp there.

Sadly I never got to the chance to use the place last year. Covid-19 restrictions meant that wild camping came to an end around that time. I was being very careful where I camped, as many small communities in the Highlands were very concerned about the risk of visitors bringing the virus with them. During that period, I continued to wild camp but made sure that any of my campsites were as far as possible from any habitation, preferably miles away.

When I return to the campsite the following winter, it appears that there has been some miscommunication between NatureScot's management in Inverness and the local folk in Torridon. Local people obviously consider the campsite closed. I don't like camping where I'm not welcome so decide that the best option is to try to find another campsite.

I look around for half an hour or so but can't find anywhere that feels right to pitch my tent. I also begin to sense that I might be starting a cold. I am feeling a little cold and a bit tired. With Omicron around I decide not to take any chances and abandon my mission. An hour later I am sitting in my centrally-heated flat beginning to feel sorry for myself. Feeling rough over the next few days does at least give me the opportunity to pen that classic of older men with nothing better to do –the complaint letter.

"Yours, Disgusted of Inverness."

I'm a relative novice at the art of complaining. Some of my friends, who have been retired a little longer than I have, have turned complaining into an art form. Martin, whom you may remember if you've read my previous books, has long been the scourge of bus and rail companies. Covid-19 allowed him to branch out into health care. The idea of having to wear a face mask appalled him so he embarked upon a letter-writing campaign, sending hundreds of letters to politicians, council administrators and anyone else unwise enough to allow their address to be publicly accessible. Martin refuses to accept modern technology so when I say letters, I don't mean emails –I mean the real thing. Manila envelopes, stamped and put into letter boxes, and actually travelling hundreds of miles to land on somebody's desk.

My friend Derek, a longstanding member of the campaign to legalise cannabis, has turned his skills to pestering the council about the quality of cycle paths. He never got that far with the cannabis campaign; even after all these years the humble weed is still illegal. The cycle paths around his home town of Norwich, on the other hand, have improved dramatically since he began hounding council officials. I like to think that people who don't work complaining about people who do work is a uniquely British cottage industry.

When I see the "Campsite Closed" sign this year I realise that my time has come. I take a photo of the offending sign so I can send it to the official in NatureScot's head office whom I wrote to previously, together with a stiff email asking for clarification of the status of the campsite during the winter months. It's pretty obvious that management have made a decision that the campsite should be open, and that the local staff at the nature reserve have decided to ignore this. I might have to harness Martin's letter writing skills after all.

My cold gradually develops from a sniffle into a full-blown coughing and spluttering snot-monster. It's obvious that I only have days to live despite the fact that numerous Covid-19 tests return negative verdicts. I follow my usual practice whenever I am ill. I google the symptoms, convince myself that only the most serious diagnoses can apply, and await death. Fortunately, the negative tests mean that Christmas can go ahead and both my daughters can stay with me, so the chocolate-eating Olympics continue in our house over the festive period while I feel sorry for myself under a mountain of tissues.

We have a great Christmas together but once my daughters have left, my flat becomes eerily quiet and I find myself wondering if I have gone deaf while I struggle to adjust back to my singleton lifestyle. The cold I contracted before Christmas decides it feels at home in my chest and refuses to budge. All thoughts of spending Hogmanay in a bothy are quickly banished and I settle into feeling miserable for the next few days.

They say you should listen to your body. I try but my body just yells, "Sausages, chips and beer." It never screams for a salad with a light vinaigrette dressing.

A few days after Christmas, I'm sitting surrounded by paracetamol and tissues when the phone rings. "Mr Burns?" a woman's voice asks.

I wonder what they are trying to sell me. "Yes?"

"Derbyshire police here. I wonder if you can help us with a missing persons enquiry?"

The young police officer explains that they are looking for a man in his mid-thirties. They are calling me because he was given a copy of my book *Bothy Tales* for Christmas, and was so inspired by it that he announced he was heading north to explore the Highlands and hasn't been heard of since. This information instantly rouses me from my stupor.

With trepidation, I ask the one question that will make all the difference to the missing man. "How experienced is he?"

"Well, he was in the army cadets when he was young," she replies.

My heart sinks –that's no experience at all. For the last few days the Highland hills have been swept by blizzards and high winds. To be out in those conditions for several days, you need to be well equipped and know what you are doing.

I probe a little. "Has he done much hillwalking?"

"We don't think so, but he's been camping in Europe," the officer says.

I cough –I'm doing a lot of that right now. The problem is that neither the officer I'm talking to nor the missing man can have any idea what he was getting into. It's not unusual for people to go missing in the Highlands. In the summer the chances of survival are good but in winter it's a different story. Most folk can survive a night, or possibly two at the most. My experience in mountain rescue tells me that the outcome for someone who has been out in bad conditions for more than a few days is unlikely to be good.

"Do you think he might have gone to one of the bothies in the book?"

"There's a good chance, but the problem is we can't get hold of a copy locally. We don't know which bothies you talk about. Can you help?"

"Yes, of course. Send me your email address and I'll send you a list of the bothies mentioned in the book."

It's more than four years since I wrote the book and I can't recall all the bothies I wrote about. I haul the little blue book out and begin to go through the chapters. It's not encouraging. The first bothy I come across is Faindouran in the eastern Cairngorms. That's a very remote place and if he's headed there under the current conditions, it will have been a long and arduous trek with serious risks. The book produces a list of fifteen bothies in all. Some are very remote, others relatively easy to reach. I've no idea if the missing man is able to tell the difference. The short December days mean that hiking to one of the remote bothies will almost certainly require navigating at night. I know only too well that it's possible to be within a hundred yards of a bothy at night and not find it.

The bothies I wrote about, fifteen in all, range right across the Highlands from Faindouran in the east to Kervaig on the windswept western tip of our islands. That is a search area the size of Belgium (I suppose that only helps you understand the scale if you know how big Belgium is). The trick, of course, will be to locate the missing man's car. Then we can narrow it down to a small area and some sort of search can begin.

At a rational level I know that this man's disappearance is not my fault. There are lots of books about mountains, and sometimes these books inspire people and some of those people lose their lives following this inspiration. I remember reading Gaston Rebuffat's *Climbing Ice* many years ago when I was living in Sheffield and beginning to dream of climbing ice. A few years later, after I had moved to Scotland, Ken Wilson's *Cold Climbs* became my bible. These books fuelled a twenty-year obsession with ice climbing that led to me ending up a thousand feet up on a Canadian ice climb with a huge avalanche doing its best to kill me and my partner. Would Ken and Gaston have been responsible for my death if luck had gone the other way? No –but despite knowing that, I feel more than a little responsible. It's my book this guy crammed into his rucksack and it's my tales that inspired this trip. I wonder if I emphasised clearly enough how difficult some of these bothies are to get to. I remember Alex suggesting to me, when he was editing the book, that I might want to include a short warning about the dangers of travelling to remote bothies. I may have been wrong to ignore his advice. I go to bed that night paying closer attention than usual to the weather forecast, with the fate of the Derbyshire walker weighing heavily on my mind.

Halfway through my porridge the following morning the phone rings.

This time it's a male colleague of the woman I spoke to last night. "We got camera footage of this guy travelling north. There is something green in the back of his car. Possibly a tent."

That footage was captured almost a week ago now. The outlook isn't good. I explain to the officer that the weather here is extreme, and if this man isn't that experienced and he's camped high up, the outlook could be serious.

"We are trying to look for his car," the policeman tells me, "but where do we start?"

He's right, the car is the key –without it, the search area is huge. "It could be anywhere. The local police should know where walkers park up."

"We were wondering if you could get the word out on social media? You probably know where to post it. I'll send you a poster."

Social media is often blamed for many ills, but if you want to get information out fast to a community there's nothing quite like it. The hope is that it will jar someone's memory. A lot of folk could have been out in the Scottish hills and one of them may have seen him. There may be someone who will know where his car is and that piece of information would be vital.

For the next three hours I pump information out across

the web. The obvious place to start is the Mountain Bothies Association Facebook page. The page has almost 20,000 members. There is a core base of users who visit bothies on a regular basis and might have spotted the missing man. Then I contact my friend, Neil Reid, who is Communications Officer for Mountaineering Scotland and he puts information about the missing man on his website. Dan Bailey, who runs UKHillWalking.com, contacts me and information goes out on their website. Then it goes up on Twitter and Instagram. In a matter of hours there can be few people in the outdoor community in Scotland, the people most likely to have information on the man from Derbyshire's whereabouts, who do not know he is missing.

I have been involved in many searches over the years, initially as a member of the Cairngorm Mountain Rescue Team and more recently simply as someone reaching out to give support to the families of missing folk or supporting the police with what little information I can give. Whenever I am involved in these situations, it always brings home to me just how unbearable it must be for those close to missing folk. The awful uncertainty, the unending pain of simply not knowing what has happened to someone you love, must be unendurable torment. As more days pass, the outcome of this search sounds increasingly uncertain and I can only imagine his family's heartache.

It's over a week since he was last seen before I'm contacted again by the police in Aviemore. The police officer this time is a Highlander and he has a very good grasp of just how serious this could be.

It's comforting to hear a Highland accent. "Can you give me the locations of these bothies? I've talked to the local rescue guys and they know the Cairngorm ones, but some of the others they've not heard of."

I hadn't realised how specialised my knowledge was. "Yes, no problem. The easiest thing for you to do is to go onto the Mountain Bothies Association website. There's a clickable map on there that will give you details of the bothies I mentioned in the book."

That's obvious to me but I realise that if you don't know this, the bothies would be time consuming to locate.

I can hear the police officer typing at the other end of the phone. "Oh right, I have it up now. That's a big help. He's been gone a while," he says, expressing his fears.

"Let's hope he's camping in the woods somewhere. I can't see how he could have spent all this time in a bothy. It would be difficult to carry enough fuel and food for this length of time."

"Yes, maybe in some sheltered spot." The officer tries to sound upbeat but I can tell that's not what he's thinking.

That afternoon I receive a message over Facebook. It's from a walker who met someone fitting the man's description near a waterfall, not far from Ben Nevis. He tells me the man seemed lost and asked for directions. It sounds an odd story because it's a long way from any of the bothies I mentioned in my book but I tell him to inform the police. There is a car park not far from the place he's talking about. Perhaps they'll find his car.

The following day I get a call from the Aviemore police officer again. They have located the missing man's car, at long last. It's nowhere near the waterfall or Ben Nevis. It's on a hill road in the Cairngorms. Although I am glad they have found the vehicle, my heart sinks. The Cairngorms can be brutal at this time of year. If you have never experienced a full-blown Cairngorm blizzard it can be difficult to imagine its ferocity. It's possible that this man has walked into the worst possible place at exactly the wrong time. I am increasingly uneasy about the situation. At least now his car has been found, the search can begin in earnest.

I'm having lunch the following day when the police call me. They have found the missing man safe and well. He was picked up by a helicopter walking out of one of the Cairngorm bothies, a bothy not mentioned in my book. He had spent some time camping in the forest through the bad weather and then decided to walk into the bothy when things improved. My sense of relief is overwhelming. I'd been more worried than I had realised. It's so wonderful to be able to put out a positive outcome on social media. The whole community allows itself a collective sigh of relief. The outcome could have been tragic. It's a good reminder to always let someone know where you are going.

A little fiction on the side. If you enjoyed *Bothy Tales*, here's a wee story you might like.

Chapter 18

Camera Trap

"I'm knackered." Bill slumped into a chair in the far corner of the bothy and began rolling a joint. "I swear that camera gets further away every time we go."

Bill always moaned about walking anywhere so Ian ignored him and felt in his pocket for the small plastic case containing the memory card.

Bill lit his spliff and inhaled slowly, relishing the heavy aroma of weed. "I'm no going next time. It does nae take two of us."

Ian flipped the lid on the laptop open and slipped the memory card in the side before lowering his lean frame onto the rough wooden chair. "You know the rules. We both have to go."

"Who's tae bloody know?" Bill snapped, belching a mouthful of smoke with each word. "This bloody bothy is miles away from anyone. There's not even a phone signal, for Christ's sake. We could take it in turns. No cunt would know."

Ian tapped the touchpad on the computer and watched as the screen came to life. "I'd know."

"For fuck's sake," Bill snarled, scratching his thick dark beard. Smoke barrelled from his nose in two parallel lines. "Ten days in this bothy's too long. No electric, no running water, no internet, no phone. It's a bloody derelict house."

"I like being here. It's peaceful up here in the hills." Ian barely looked up from the glowing screen.

Bill grunted. "You can keep 'peaceful'. I could be home with the widescreen watching the footie. If they didn't pay so well to look for the damn cats, I'd be out of here I can tell you."

The pair fell silent, the tension between them filling the room as the light from the bothy window caught the smoke from Bill's joint. Ian watched as the icons for each short video on the memory card appeared.

"Are there many?" Bill asked as he rose from the armchair.

Ian scrolled to the bottom of the screen. "One hundred and fourteen."

"Oh, for fuck's sake. Youse are welcome to that." Bill stomped across the room and headed for the kitchen, calling over his shoulder as he went, "You want some tea?"

Ian sighed. Bill always calmed down after a few minutes and a joint. By three in the afternoon Bill got twitchy, needing his first blast of weed. At first Ian had found that irritating but now he just accepted it. Bill couldn't function without weed –that was the way it was.

Ian clicked on the first twenty-second video the camera trap had shot. Nothing moved in it. The log leaned at an angle and the bait sat untouched. He watched another six videos. Same thing –nothing moved. That was the trouble with camera traps: too sensitive. The slightest movement could set off the motion sensors or a tiny change in temperature caused by the sun on the log could trigger the heat sensor. Nothing else for it, just got to go through all of them, one by one.

Twelve slides in, he caught a movement in one of the videos. Perhaps it was an ear, possibly a leaf. As he watched, something moved on the edge of the frame. There was definitely something slightly out of shot. Ian held his breath. A roe deer walked over to the log and sniffed at the bait.

"Shit." Ian allowed himself the little curse. Bill's constant trickle of obscenities made Ian want to swear less, but every once in a while he let himself use a profanity. If you swear all the time, he'd said to Bill, what's left to say when things are really bad? Bill had shrugged his shoulders, cursed again, and taken another pull of weed. There was no reasoning with the man.

A mug of tea, attached to Bill's arm, arrived next to the computer. "What is it?"

"Roe deer." Ian yawned.

Bill plodded over to his seat. "It's always roe deer." For once he didn't swear.

"Or squirrels."

Bill laughed. "Oh aye, I forgot about the squirrels."

Or maybe the wind, or a blue tit, Ian thought, or any one of the hundred things he'd seen trigger the camera over the last month. Sometimes it was nothing at all.

A beer can opened with a hiss from Bill's corner. "I'm needing this, I can tell you." Bill poured half the contents of a can of Punk IPA craft beer down his throat in one go. The heady scent of it filled the room.

Ian was about to open the next video when the low-charge warning popped up on his laptop. "Oh no, now the power's gone."

"It'll be that connection again. Needs checking." Bill didn't move. He was in the process of rolling another joint and it was obvious he had no intention of going anywhere.

Ian sighed and rose from the computer. Outside the bothy the summer sun was still high in the sky. It would be another hour before it dipped below the hills, then the air would grow cool and they would have to light the wood-burning stove. As Ian crossed the few hundred yards of rough ground between the small stone dwelling and the bank of photoelectric cells, he could already feel the chill in the air.

The network of cells was around twenty feet long and half as high. The weather had been good and there had been plenty of sun all through the six weeks that he and Bill had been working on the project, so the cells should have been producing power. Ian knelt behind the cells and picked up the wire that led back to the bothy. He unwound the gaffer tape and pushed the two metal sections of the connector together. Ian looked back at the doorway of the stone cottage nestling beneath the green hills. The door opened and Bill's stocky bearded figure emerged, beer in one hand and joint in the other. Bill grinned and gave a thumbs up, calling something indecipherable. Ian laughed, pleased that Bill had managed to rise from his chair long enough to check that the current was flowing.

For the next hour and half Ian checked through the videos captured by the camera. Most had nothing in them save the log and its bait but Ian had to watch them all in case there was a sign of a cat. By now Bill, several cans and a number of joints into his evening relaxation, was snoring in his chair. As he started to check the last twenty or so videos, getting into night shots now, Ian realised he was beginning to feel hungry. He glanced at the time and saw it was six fifteen.

"Bill! Bill!"

Bill opened one eye. "What?"

"It's gone six."

Instantly Bill began to simultaneously rouse himself and reach for his jacket. "For Christ's sake, why didn't you tell me?"

"It's not my fault if you get tanked up and then spark out, is it?"

Bill had his jacket on by now and was heading for the door. "She'll want to know why I'm late. I'll tell her it's your fault."

Ian smiled. "Send Beth my love."

"Piss off." Bill headed off for his twenty-minute walk up the hill to find phone signal and call Beth, his wife. This was his daily ritual. Ian realised long ago that for all Bill's macho brashness, he was devoted to his wife. Even when rain swept down the glen and battered the bothy roof, he would pull on his waterproofs and set off to make the call, despite muttering obscenities at having to perform the duty. It was all an act; he was desperate to talk to her. In the rough room where they slept, Bill had stuck a picture of himself and Beth taken only a few weeks before their wedding three years ago. It was taken in some pub –Ian couldn't remember which one. She was dressed in a simple print dress and looked pretty. She had beautiful blue eyes, dark hair tied back and a big open smile on her face. Ian remembered the day well. Beth was looking out of the picture with her head slightly tilted, the way she often did. Bill looked more than a little drunk and had his arm draped heavily around her shoulders and a big grin on his face. He might look a bit of an oaf, but no one who looked at that photograph could be in any doubt that Bill was as in love as it was possible to be.

Ian clicked on the next video clip but only half watched it. He was growing bored and wondered just how many clips he'd watched over the time he and Bill had been setting the camera traps. Then a movement on the video caught his eye. It was on the edge of the screen and only appeared in shot for a split second, but it looked like an arm. A human arm. Ian checked the time. 3:34 a.m. He replayed the video, and after a few attempts he was able to freeze the image just as the arm appeared. It was a grainy shot. Perhaps it was an arm, or maybe it was something else.

"Who would be there at that time of night?" Ian muttered to himself.

The camera was buried in the forest, a long way up the glen

beyond the bothy. He and Bill had been there hundreds of times but sometimes, if the mist was down, even they had to double-check how to get there. Ian watched the video over again. When he froze the frame, whatever was in the image looked less like an arm. Maybe he was imagining things. When he played the video again, he realised it was more the way whatever it was moved that made him think it could be somebody's arm.

Ian watched the remainder of the videos but saw nothing unusual. At one point a badger tried to climb the log to get at the bait. He failed because it was too steep. It was deliberately set that way so that was nothing unusual.

The bothy door rattled and Bill walked in, looking happier now he'd spoken to Beth.

"Take a look at this," Ian blurted out as Bill unzipped his jacket.

Bill's eyes brightened. "Jesus, don't tell me we've got a lynx at last?"

Bill was already bending over Ian's shoulder, staring at the screen. Ian shook his head. "No, not a lynx. It looks like somebody's arm."

Bill ran his fingers through his thick dark hair, looking puzzled. "Arm?"

Ian pressed play. "Well, it could be."

Bill squinted at the laptop screen. He could see the log leant against the stump, and the small tray of bait halfway along its length. Then something moved in the corner of the screen. "Is that it?"

Ian nodded.

Bill sighed and sat down in his chair. "That's no an arm," he said, dismissively.

"Well, tell me what it is then!" Ian snapped back.

Bill was already rolling another spliff. "It'll be a roe deer."

Ian looked at the image again

The shape was blurred, Perhaps it was too close to the camera. Ian played it twice more. He felt sure there was something human about the movement on the screen.

Bill was methodically laying out his weed, tobacco and cigarette pieces. The burly Glaswegian was careless and clumsy about everything he did except his joint rolling. About that, he was meticulous. "I wonder if we'll ever see a lynx. Three months since the tracking collars packed up. No one on this project has caught so much as a glimpse."

Ian snapped the laptop shut and almost raised his voice. "They're here. I'm sure of that."

Bill licked the cigarette paper and expertly rolled a joint and closed it in one adept movement. If he sensed the anger in Ian's mood, he didn't show it. "Ah well, you're the zoology professor. I'm just here to make sure you don't fall down a hole. What would I know?"

Ian sat watching the camera shots over again. "It does look like an arm."

Bill blew a lung full of smoke across the floor and eased himself back into his chair. "Ach you're seeing things. People say the camera never lies, but it lies all the time."

Their last three days in the glen were uneventful. The weather broke, filling the coire above and the woods below with a soft rain, misting the air and shrinking the world to the few hundred yards between them and the dank walls of low cloud. On days like these the wet seeped into everything. The bothy stank of damp and even the stove couldn't dry the place out. Bill became increasingly morose, counting down the nights until he could get home and rationing the last of his beers.

On the final day of their shift, Bill rushed about collecting his belongings and packing them away into his rucksack and a big red waterproof grip. "Have you seen my mp3 player?"

Bill was always looking for something. He lost things all the time.

Ian was finishing his porridge. Without looking up, he pointed to the mantlepiece above the old black iron stove.

"Oh Christ, there it is." Bill stuffed the small silver player into a rucksack pocket and zipped it closed.

Ian savoured the last mouthful of porridge, then sighed and leant back in his chair. "Of course, the chopper might not get in, what with the mist."

Bill rushed to the window and peered out into the grey wall of rain. "Oh Christ, don't say that. I'm going stir crazy here."

Ian smiled to himself. It was difficult to resist teasing Bill sometimes. "Relax, they'll be here in an hour or so."

~

It was two weeks later, while Bill was out calling Beth, that Ian first saw the woman on the screen of the laptop. She was standing with her back to the camera looking at the log. The shot on the camera card was taken in the early hours of the morning but the night vision picked her up. It wasn't clear, but you could tell it was a woman. In the pitch dark she had walked through the woods and spent almost ten seconds staring at the log. Hard to say how old she was, anything from seventeen to forty, but she was there alright.

Bill came back into the bothy, noisy and blundering about as usual. "Bastard horsefly got me on the arm while I was talking. Right through my bloody shirt."

Ian didn't answer. He sat staring at the screen.

Bill noticed Ian's tension and realised something unusual had happened. "What is it?"

Ian swivelled the laptop round so Bill could see the screen. "You'd better see this."

"Bloody hell." Bill watched the shot three times over. "Three a.m.!"

Ian nodded slowly. "Pitch dark. How could she even find it in the dark?"

"Who is she?" Bill looked hard at the screen.

Some faded memory stirred in Ian's mind. Something in the way the woman stood.

The next day when they went up to the camera trap, they searched for any signs or traces of the woman.

Bill stared at the ground where she had stood. "There's nae marks. Not a blade of grass has been moved. Nothing."

"Weird." Ian joined him and peered into the bushes.

"There'd be a mark." Bill was confident of his tracking

abilities. "A footprint. The grass flattened. Something."

"Maybe she came in a different way."

"There is nae other way." Bill waved at the thick forest around them. "I don't like this."

Ian could see Bill was shaken. "Maybe it's some eco warrior girl looking for the lynx."

Bill snorted and pointed to the ground. "Aye, who can fly. Let's get out of here."

Bill was quiet in the bothy that night. No joints. He just sat and stared until it was time to phone Beth.

When he came back from his call, he was agitated. "I've got to go home. Something's come up."

"What—"

Bill cut him off. "I've got to go. I'll walk out. If I'm quick, I'll catch the bus from the end of the glen. Hitch, even."

In ten minutes Bill was gone. He had thrown a handful of things into his rucksack and marched off down the glen.

In the silence of the bothy Ian watched the video of the woman over and over. There was still something familiar about her but he couldn't work out what. Something about the way she held herself perhaps. He couldn't see her clearly enough in the night vision.

The next day Ian walked up the glen alone. It was warm, and a gentle breeze kept the midges and horseflies at bay. He should have phoned the office but the project manager wouldn't be too impressed by Bill storming off, and he didn't want to get Bill into more trouble than he was already in. There was no ghost girl on the tape from last night. Ian was relieved if he was honest. The thought of a woman wandering the woods in the darkness while he slept wasn't the best way to lull himself to sleep.

On his way back to the bothy, Ian detoured the few hundred yards to the small hillock where it was possible to get a phone signal. He dialled Bill's number. The phone rang for a while and then went to answerphone. There was a sudden stab of pain in Ian's left arm. He looked down and saw a horsefly biting into his arm.

Back at the bothy, Ian began to tidy up. Bill had left his jacket hung over the chair and when Ian picked it up, something metallic fell from one of the pockets and clattered under a chair.

"Oh, damn." Ian bent to reach under the chair, fumbling for the object. His fingertips found something smooth and he pulled it out. It was Bill's phone.

Ian looked at it in disbelief. Bill was always casual about his things but leaving his phone was incredibly careless, even for him. Ian glanced at the screen. No calls. How could there be any –there was no signal in the bothy. He put the phone down and started setting the stove and putting the kettle on. He hardly dared to admit it but he was beginning to miss Bill's grumpy presence. The bothy wasn't the same without the smell of weed. Ian went over to Bill's beer store, opened a can and sat down. Another long night.

By the next morning Ian had made a decision. He couldn't cover for Bill any longer. He would walk over to the small hill where he could get phone reception. By now Bill would have realised he'd left his phone and tried to call him, perhaps letting him know when he'd be coming back.

Ian was walking up the small hill when he realised he was sweating. He was rushing. Why, when there was no urgency in this? He had a sudden sense that something was wrong. He pulled his phone out, except it wasn't his phone –he found Bill's in his hand. Bill never locked his phone, claiming it was too much trouble. Ian switched the phone on and waited while it beeped with two days of texts and emails. But there were no missed calls. No messages from Beth.

Call Beth. That's what he should do. Bill would be with her and then they could try to sort this out. If Bill came back now, they could keep his brief absence from the job to themselves. Ian opened Bill's phone. There was Beth smiling from the contacts list. Ian fumbled with the phone and opened the recent calls list by accident. The list was empty. No daily calls to Beth at six o'clock. In fact, no calls at all. Ian stood, puzzling at the absence of calls, when he felt a sharp pain in his arm.

He slapped his elbow. "Bastard!" A horsefly dropped into the grass, dead.

Ian called Beth. A man's voice answered, furious. "Where the fuck are you? Tell me, you bastard. Tell me!"

Ian hung up without answering. There had been desperation in that voice, he thought, perhaps even fear. One thing he was certain of: it wasn't Beth or Bill. He stood staring at the phone trying to decide if the voice was familiar. Try as he could, he couldn't place the person on the other end.

The phone came to life with a raucous burst of banjo playing, Bill's annoying ring tone. It was Beth's number. Ian hesitated, his finger hovering over the green answer button. If he answered he'd become inextricably entangled in whatever was going on with Bill and Beth. He listened to few more jarring banjo chords before he switched the phone off and slipped it in his pocket. He didn't want to know what was going on and he didn't need to.

He turned his own phone on and watched the missed calls come pinging in. None of the calls could be from Bill –he knew everyone who called him. Reluctantly, he called the office and got hold of his boss. There was silence on the phone while Ian explained what had happened. He knew what was coming: don't go to the camera site alone. Stay in the bothy. Follow health and safety. Chopper in tomorrow to either replace Bill or take Ian out.

"Okay, yes. Okay. I understand," he heard himself saying.

Back in the bothy, he lit the small gas ring and watched the steam rise from the kettle. Might as well check out last night's camera card. It would be some consolation if he spotted a lynx on what was probably his last night in the glen. The first thirty files showed nothing but the baited log and one shot of a badger trying to steal the bait. Then he saw her coming out of the darkness. The young woman. She turned towards the camera and her eyes shone in the reflected light.

Ian tried to search her features but the image was too dark. He searched the next ten files. Nothing.

He was finishing his tea when a thought crossed his mind:

the video editing software. It might help him to see her better.

He took the file with the image of the woman, waited until she was fully in shot and then turned the brightness right up. Beth's face stared back at him out of the screen. She was looking at something out of shot, her head slightly to one side in that way she had.

Ian began searching the other video clips. Beth was in all of them, alone at first, and then a man entered the shot. He was only there for a second and Ian didn't recognise him.

Then he watched the last video file.

Beth was standing with her back to the log and staring at something beyond the camera. Then Bill's thick-set figure walked into shot. He and Beth argued. Ian turned up the sound, but all he could make out was muffled voices. The argument was escalating. Then, Bill raised his arm and lashed out. Beth went down. Bill turned, wrenched the camera from its mounting. Blackness.

By the time he reached the path through the forest to the camera, Ian was blowing hard and sweating. He pushed his way through the forest, his stomach churning. Ian walked into the clearing. There was the baited log, same as it always was. Ian looked at the grass beneath the log. No sign of anyone being there and, most important of all, no Beth. Ian leant against the log. He realised his legs were shaking but the fear had gone from him. He had half-expected to find Beth lying beside the log. That seemed ridiculous now.

Ian turned and reached for the camera, and there was Bill. He was eight feet from the ground, his body hanging from a tree, swinging gently in the warm breeze.

Book 3
Secret Places

Climb the mountains and get their good tidings. Nature's peace will flow into you as sunshine flows into trees. The winds will blow their own freshness into you, and the storms their energy, while cares will drop away from you like the leaves of Autumn.

John Muir

Chapter 19

The Tales of the Land

At the end of the year, I managed to contract a cold that seemed to come and go all through January. My Covid-19 tests all came back negative but every time I thought the cold had left me and tried to go for a walk, it returned with added vengeance. I spent weeks in enforced idleness.

About this time, I got a commission to write a poem for the Spirit 360 project which is working to repurpose Inverness Castle. If you've visited Inverness, you'll know that the skyline is dominated by a Victorian sandstone castle with mock turrets and castellated walls. There have been castles on this site, overlooking the town, for over a thousand years. Several of these were blown up or burnt down during the tempestuous history of the Highlands. The current castle served as the Highland Capital's Law Courts until only a few years ago, when that function was moved to a purpose-built court centre handily situated next door to the police station.

The current plan is to turn the old castle into a state-of-the-art visitor centre to showcase the Highlands and to rehouse Inverness Museum. As part of that project I was offered a commission to produce any work of my choice. I decided to write something from the perspectives of the climbers and walkers who wander the Highlands which would also say something about what we have done to the land and how the animals that once lived here could return.

This is the poem I wrote.

The Tales of the Land

These are the stories of the hills.
Tales of the high peaks and deep glens,
ragged white foamed shores
and silent moss dark forests.
These are the tales of the land
told by its Pagan-hearted people.
These are the stories of those who scale the wild cliffs,
and walk long lonely ridges.
Whispered in candlelit bothies, they are sung by the rocks
and the ruined township walls.
These are the lives of those who love the untamed places.

We are of the land beneath our feet.
The blood of the earth flows within us.
Its song is ours too.
For those who listen the sky talks,

and there is music in the wild wind.
The old life in us longs to embrace the land,
to roam these Highlands that lent us life.
The land brims with stories of the folk it has known,
of the people who spend their lives amongst its hills and glens.
It speaks of the people it has lost and cries for the dispossessed.
It sings for the walkers and the climbers,
For those that love it still.
The rocks and the tumbling waters recall the forests
and search for those who are missing.
They ache for the soft footed lynx.
They long for the grey slinking wolves
that slipped away, like smoke through the trees, moments ago.
We are the creatures of the land,
we are its children.
Come closer, I have tales to tell.

The Climber's Tale

My dreams are born in high places.
They come from the ageless cliffs,
the soaring rock and the vast beckoning below.
Here I test my sinew, my courage, skill and hope
in this arena of truth.
My tale is written by fingertips on jagged edges,
I am a priest in a vertical temple.
I sing of my faith on overhangs and chimneys
with hands wedged in cracks and feet smeared on hope.
I trust the god of gravity and pray for his forgiveness.

In these places, where few can linger,

I found brothers and sisters and we formed our church of this
    improbable brotherhood.

Together we gloried in our victories and laughed at our failures,

Even though they cut us deep.

We struggled, pushed, swung and scrambled.

knew fear, hope, despair and joy.

In these tall places we left the drab

monotone days spent toiling to feed the machine.

For a fraction we lived in Technicolour,

our lives stripped down, destiny in our hands.

Our zen the joy of movement, the freedom of a body in space.

In summer my story is told on warm slabs,

Balanced as delicate as a moth's wing.

When winter comes the song changes

and is sung in the shattered ice of frozen starlight.

Moments caught in the breath and felt in a heartbeat.

We reach the summit of these frozen places as darkness falls

And see the lights of life twinkling below

Knowing that for a few moments we dwelt in an exalted place.

And yes, there were times we watched in silence

as those who paid the mountain's toll

came slowly down in stillness,

our hearts emptying for them.

We learned from these great places how fragile we are.

We felt fools, became lost and found ourselves again.

We laughed at our follies, came swinging off the cliffs on taut ropes
cracking our pride and our knees
and learning to laugh at both.
Yet still we tell the climber's tale
For it is our song of life and joy, a dream of tactile things.

The Hillwalker's Tale

My legs are weary, feet sore, ankles aching.
I am burnt by the sun and blasted by the wind.
Yet I climb higher still, searching the endless horizon.
A moment ago I left the valley
and headed upwards into this ancient place.
Here the earth sings beneath my feet
as I gaze across a limitless land.

I am far travelled yet rest is forbidden.
I seek these hills for here is my home.
Once I lost my way in city streets and grey built towns,
Amongst factories and sightless offices.
My vacant eyes watching endless screens,
Listening to the babble of empty words.
I stared at these illusions so long I forgot how to see
until a distant whisper called me back to these forsaken places.

I have seen the spindrift whip across Cairngorm summit
and the sunrise in Glen Coe as the icy tops catch fire.
I have walked alone yet felt a spirit with me.
I stood staring in wonder at wild Lochnagar,

while in my heart dreams of these places grew.
Here I listened only to the wind and let my heart sing.
In these hills I have wandered the long day
Regretting that this time will ever end.
I felt the harsh hail and the warm sun,
the gentle rain and the angry wind,
knowing that these were the moods of an old friend.

I wander distant places and see the seasons turning.
In spring as winter loses its ice fast grip
I feel the earth stirring as the force of life
writhes impatient to escape the cold cocoon.
Winter's grip must yield to the quickening pulse of Spring.
In the forest the desiccated tones of yellow and brown
give way to the green of life as leaves burst open.
At last the silence of the frigid air yields to the song of birds.
In nests perfect eggs crack open
And are filled with the gapping mouths of insistent chicks.
I watch the hen harrier sweep across the waving grass,
on ghost white wings he flashes over the rolling ground
seeking prey to feed his broods of hungry chicks.
A survivor of the assassins, he is a prayer of hope.

When the long languid days of summer came
I spent my days on the hills and glens
and leant against the rowan as the sun warmed the earth.
On days like these, when the air beats with a billion insect wings,
I feel the pulse of the land as the long summer sits luxuriant.

September brings the first touch of autumn with splashes of
    gold among the trees.
It's then that the pace quickens in the children of the glen,
as all life races to brace itself for the coming cold.
The trees draw in the blood from their leaves
Ready for the dark gales coming.
All life knows that the dance of summer is ended
and the chill of the short days and ice winds is coming.
Now the forests bloom with colours of gold and russet brown.
For these few weeks the woodland hills burn in glorious colour
until the autumnal gales leave the woods black veined
    skeletons against grey skies.
Soon the ice of winter stills the glen
and holds it tight in immovable chill,
as the earth bends its head and bows before the harsh cold.
The cycle goes on, change and chill, sun and wind.
The seasons march brings life to this eternal land.
It is here I walk, my existence running its long season
until I return to the earth as winter comes once more.

The Bothy's Tale

Walk along the old footworn path.
Follow the giggling burn through the oak wood
to where it forces its way between the stubborn rocks,
Its water white with the scent of heather and wind.
Here the trout jigs between the stones,
the water is quick with a thousand lives,
and the creaking bridge speaks of footsteps.

Higher still, leave the wizened trees
and step into the open glen where silence booms across the land.
Amongst these far hills you will find me
in the kingdom of the stag and the eagle.
At the foot of the ridge where the hills sweep down
embracing the valley like a lost friend,
I sit and wait to welcome you.
I am the bothy that shelters from the rain.
My walls have stood against these winds a hundred years
and will stand a hundred more.

In the dark of my walls rucksacks empty.
Coal and candles, mugs and plates,
Food and whisky, tumble onto my floor
as night creeps in over the hills.
Only the phantom wings of the owl move now.
My old stone walls are cold,
and the room peat dark.

A match, a spark, and a candle flickers.
In the hearth kindling comes alive
and the reluctant coals smoke a while
until the yellow flames begin to dance.
Now, with life beneath my roof I breathe again
remembering those I sheltered long ago.
Once there was a family here.
Once children were born and grew
to laugh around my rowan tree.

Once a woman toiled to hold back the soot and the dirt
To keep her children clean and fed.
No one lives here now
but for a while my walls are home again to travellers of these hills.

There are voices and laughter.
Stories are told, as strangers become friends.
Leaving the troubles of their lives far away.
Davie sings as Tam plays his harmonica.
Jenny tells her story of a night lost on the mountain.
All are equal within my walls.
I shelter these folk and care not who they are.
I see no foreigners or foes,
Only folk who sit a while beside my hearth
And take a little warmth in a cold world.

The Eagle's Tale

I am wind. I am of air and open sky.
Wing borne, free of the tethers of earth
I roll among the tumbling clouds.
My flight is timeless in these boundless skies.
Far above this green raked country
I look down upon the flesh of the land,
its ice etched bones rolling on below.

My eyes are bright and see beyond.
I see the small creatures and the marks of time.
Once I soared over forests.

I watched the elk and the buffalo,
saw the grey wolf, a ghost among the trees.
I witnessed a bear take a silver fish bleeding from the river.
I watched as the forests fell and burnt
when the dark smoke fills the sky.
Those things are remembered by these mountains,
The earth does not forget.
Only the bones remain, scoured of their flesh.
This land is empty and aches for those it has lost.
Yet even now the land burns, and its creatures suffer
at the hands of men who rake the sky with claws of lead
and count death among their pleasures.
There is sorrow in my flight as I turn towards white capped sea
and leave behind this scar wracked land.

The Tale of the Stone

One autumn day I took the steep track into the forest.
I walked up through the scented pines.
I followed an old way to where the ground levels.
On to where the trees give way to the open glen
and the river runs clear across a bed of painted stones.
Here I left the darkness of the forest and walked in the sunlight.
There is a silence here that hangs in the air.
It is the timeless quiet of a land holding its breath.

Alone in this voiceless place I found them.
A line of stones here, and there a fallen lintel sunk with age,
tumbled into the long grass like a lost memory.

All that is left of lives that once were lived here.
I laid my hand on the rough stone and felt its memories.
A red haired girl ran here once,
With the unhindered joy of childhood.
A young man toiled in this field
until time came to dim his eyes and bend his back.
He lies there, beneath the twisted rowan.
These are the echoes of a place that has lost its folk.
They are not forgotten, these stones remember
the people who lived here once, and the life that was lost.

The Cry of the Land

My voice is silence, my words are still,
yet I am speaking now.
In the corners of the land the forest is creeping back,
tiptoeing in to claim the empty glens.
Where the stream runs between the lochs
there are marks on the trees not seen for centuries.
They were made by beavers come to shape the water.
In time they will change the course of the river
And give new life the chance it needs.

I wait for a sign to let me heal.
To bring back the forests
and let the leaping fish return to the rivers.
I have not forsaken this land.
For I am old enough to forgive
if you are wise enough to listen.

Chapter 20

Did Someone Cough?

It's a few days into the new year of 2022 and I am standing outside a large supermarket on the outskirts of Inverness. You know what is about to happen less than two months from now. Happily, at this moment I am totally unaware that Putin is about to threaten to turn us all into dust, so my main concern is trying to get over the cold that has stopped me from going anywhere for the last three weeks. I know it's a cold because I've taken several thousand Covid-19 tests over the last few days. Right now I feel uncomfortable if there *isn't* something up my nose. I know I have a cold but I am acutely aware that the folk around me, hidden behind their blue face masks, don't know that. I mustn't cough.

I get round the supermarket as fast as I can. During the drive here I was coughing so hard I almost drove off the road but I'm hoping that, at least for a while, I've coughed myself out. So far, so good. I've filled my trolley with the essentials of life and I haven't alarmed the populace by coughing once. All I need now is a few tins of beans and then I can head for the checkout and make my escape. I'm just reaching out for one of those multipacks of low-sugar baked beans when I feel a slight tickle in my throat. Time to go.

I'm lucky. There is only one person in front of me, a middle-aged woman with a great pile of groceries. Fortunately, the young, blonde checkout girl has already scanned most of them and the woman is searching in her bag for her purse. It's now that the slight tickle in the back of my throat begins to be more insistent. I emit a sort of grunt rather than a cough. The checkout girl glances up from her till and looks at me suspiciously from behind her mask and her plastic screen. Perhaps she can tell I'm suffering from some sort of cold. If I was her, meeting hundreds of people a day, I think I'd be hyper-sensitive to anyone with any sign of the sniffles.

As the woman in front of me fumbles with her purse, the urge to cough rises up inside me like a genie furiously trying to escape its lamp. My lungs start to strain as I desperately try to hold the cough in. I am certain, after all my tests, that all I have is a cold but I doubt the shoppers around me would feel as confident as I am. By now my chest is heaving and the checkout girl is looking at me very hard. I have to control my heaving chest.

It's my turn now and the young woman on the checkout starts scanning my groceries.

She glances up at me. "Have you been busy today?"

The poor woman must have been on some terrible corporate torture course where they taught her that not only did she have to spend hours of her life scanning tins of soup, but she was also supposed to be interested in the lives of her customers.

"No, not really." Before I even get to the end of the sentence I realise that attempting to speak is a big mistake. I can no longer control the beast in my chest and issue forth a huge spluttering cough. The checkout girl visibly shrinks behind her screen.

"It's alright, I've been tested," I wheeze. "It's not Cov-Cov-Covid!" Trying to repress my instinct to cough seems to have only created some sort of mucus logjam. Now the dam has burst and a tidal wave of coughing has me bent over, eyes streaming and struggling to breathe. The checkout girl is so low down in her cubicle that I can only see her eyes above the till, peering at me in obvious alarm. The folk at the adjacent tills are shrinking away. One woman with an infant in a pushchair wheels him hurriedly behind the cigarette kiosk. I manage to stand just as an elderly free church minister, two checkouts along, decides that he'll give the good Lord a helping hand in saving him and breaks into a sprint. For an old man carrying two large shopping bags, he shows a remarkable athleticism and is out of the supermarket doors in seconds.

I've given up all attempts at pretending not to cough as the assistant hurls my shopping into the trolley and thrusts the card device towards me, carefully holding it at arm's length. The whole supermarket has stopped, customers and assistants alike peering from behind the shelves as if the Angel of Death had just popped into the store to pick up his weekly order of nerve agent. The assistant starts wildly spraying her counter with anti-bacterial spray. Not content with killing anything that may have settled on the counter, she sprays into the air, trying to shoot down any of my germs that may still be parachuting down onto her. Still spluttering, I rush from the store.

My cold lasts well into January. I can't believe it's not Covid-19 but all my tests come back negative. It's not a severe cold, but it's enough to take me out for the whole of January. My only consolation is that the weather is pretty grim. Successive fronts sweep in from the Atlantic bringing wind and rain. Even had I been well, I don't think I would have been able to achieve much.

Chapter 21
Miracle in the North

Fast forward about two months, to the beginning of March. The slight non-Covid-19 cough has never really got very serious, but it hasn't gone away either. I keep feeling okay, convince myself I'm over it and head out on my bike or try and go into the hills. Every time, I find myself coughing and breathless, realising that I am far from being over this weird malady. By the end of January I am almost better, then the weather decides not to co-operate and we are hit by storm after storm with almost constant high winds. Eventually, when I've almost given up any chance of seeing a winter at all, things start to improve in March and then –a miracle happens.

I've been to Achnanclach bothy many times over the years. I like going there because it's only a short walk in and, no matter how foul the weather is, you are likely to get there in one piece. It is also in Sutherland, and I never lose my fascination for that great northern landscape, with its atmosphere of wildness and vast stretches of open land. The bothy is a low stone cottage, hiding itself away so well on the hillside that it is not until you are a few feet away that it pops up out of the landscape like a magician's assistant leaping from an empty box.

"See, I was here all the time," it seems to say.

One of the things I love about this bothy is the incredible view from the little shelter's doorway. The bothy sits high on a north-facing hill. As you lean against the bothy door, the rugged prow of Ben Loyal, to the west, cuts into the moorland below, with clouds racing across the mountain's summit. To the north a rolling area of moorland slopes gently away into an uninhabited landscape of lochs and rolling grassland. This moorland is a huge area of deep peat, known as the Flow Country, which extends for some 1,500 square miles across Sutherland and on into Caithness. It is the largest area of blanket bog in Europe. Its name comes from the Old Norse of the Vikings who once colonised these lands. They used the word "floi", meaning wet or marsh. The land is characterised by an endless mosaic of pools and grasslands and is largely devoid of trees. This is a habitat that offers a home to a wide variety of birds including the much-persecuted hen harrier.

For some, this landscape would be featureless and bleak, devoid of interest –somewhere to be shunned. For me it has the timeless beauty of a landscape that has remained unchanged for thousands of years. The only sounds here are the endless winds and the calls of the plover and the stone chat. Only moments ago, the longboats sailed out of the estuary and set their sails for history.

Returning to this bothy is like coming home. I settle into

a familiar routine, eating a simple meal and lighting the candles and the coal fire. As the yellow flames begin to dance and the light of the day fades, I settle down for the evening, laying my sleeping bag out on the small platform beside the fire. The evening slips away in silence. I enjoy a little whisky and spend my time watching the fire dance and dreaming. About ten o'clock, I decide it is bedtime and head outside for a pee. Then a miracle occurs.

In the cold wind, beyond the bothy door, something magical has occurred. The night is so bright that the landscape is illuminated as if it were daytime, and I can walk around without any need of my torch. The moon is almost full and shines down on the hillside from a clear sky dotted with thousands of stars. This would be enough of a wonder, but across the rolling moor the sky is dancing. Great columns of white ghost-like lights shimmer and shift in the sky. I stare in awe as the aurora borealis commands the night sky.

I have travelled these Highland bothies for almost forty years yet, in all that time, this sight has eluded me. I have only seen the northern lights in faint glimpses on the horizon or, more often than not, I have missed them totally. I've always been in the wrong bothy, or in the right bothy at the wrong time. Once I was even in the right bothy at the right time but looking out of the wrong window. Now at last, by a fluke of luck, I am in the perfect place.

Most things that you anticipate for a long time are a disappointment when they finally arrive. Meals are not as tasty; a comedian you had wanted to see for years was not quite as funny as you had hoped. The aurora borealis does not fall into that category. It is a truly amazing sight, far more spectacular than I had imagined. I had thought that the northern lights would occupy only a small section of the night sky but the display is vast, occupying half the heavens. The sky shimmers and shakes. Vast towers of light appear solid for a few seconds and then sink back into an unseen world of shadows. A chasm into a parallel world opens up and I can see unimaginable things.

It is far more spectacular than any man-made fireworks display I have ever seen. Achnanchlach bothy is the perfect place to watch from. There is no light pollution here so from where I stand, shivering in the bothy doorway, I am looking out onto a primeval scene. The sky above dances with light, and the huge expanse of bog that is the Flow Country stretches below. This scene has played out countless times and the spectacle would have been identical ten thousand years ago. Viking warriors looked up from their night fires and gazed in awe at this sight, just as I do now. For the Vikings, this eerie display was the reflection from the shields of the warrior women –Valkyrie, the choosers of the slain, who decided who lived and died in battle. They guarded the light bridge that allowed those who had died to pass over into Valhalla. Looking into the sky on this night, it is easy to believe this is the route to heaven.

I never sought to see the aurora. I thought that if I travelled to remote bothies frequently enough, I would eventually see them without having to make a special effort. Now that I realise what an incredible sight they are, I will make it my business to track them whenever I can. They are more than just a sight; watching them is to experience what the essence of the north is, a glimpse into the soul of this landscape.

I am surprised that the aurora appears mostly white. Many photographs I've seen show vivid greens and reds. I wonder if the bright moonlight has somehow washed out the colours.

Later, when I am back in Inverness, I contact Chris Cooke to find an answer to the question of the colours. Chris and I have known each other since our university days in Leicester, when we shared a flat and an abiding interest in real ale. Since then we had lost contact with each other, until he suddenly turned up on Facebook, living in the Cayman Islands. He's now moved back to the UK and we have met up on a few occasions. Chris studied astrophysics at university and is still keenly interested in all things celestial. He gives talks on astronomy and is in demand in the Plymouth area, where he now lives. Chris has one of the most expensive hobbies in existence, if you consider it on a time-to-activity ratio. He is an eclipse chaser and has travelled all over the world trying to put himself in the path of total solar eclipses. As that has taken him to places like Mexico and Arizona, and eclipses only last for around six minutes, the cost per second of this activity must be astronomical, if you'll excuse the pun. I know that Chris has travelled to Iceland to see the aurora borealis. While that counts as cheating in my book, I know he is the best person to explain what I'd seen. He is very interested to hear of my northern encounter.

"Ah, well," Chris's disembodied head says from the other

end of a Zoom call, "The effect is caused by a geomagnetic storm entering the Earth's atmosphere, driven by solar winds."

"Oh, right. I see." I don't. I have some idea what a geomagnetic storm might be but solar winds are beyond my understanding. "But it's not green?"

Chris is warming to his subject now. "When you witness the northern lights with the naked eye they are mostly white. There are some faint colours. Modern cameras pick up colours that our eyes can't, so when you take pictures the lights appear more colourful than they are to the naked eye."

"Ah, right. It's a pity I didn't take photos. I just didn't think my phone camera would be able to do anything with it."

Chris grins at me through the screen, evidently happy to see how impressed I am by this astronomical phenomenon. "I can always tell when someone has actually seen something. When I show people a distant galaxy they often sort of casually say that they have seen it –then I know they haven't. But when their voice is full of awe, I know they have really seen it."

He's seen my reaction. "Well, I really saw it."

Chris laughs. "I can tell."

I try to avoid giving advice but I'm going to make an exception here: if you get a chance to see the aurora borealis, take it. I'm hooked now and will be hunting them down whenever I get a chance.

227

In Achnanchlach bothy, the morning after seeing the northern lights, the sky is clear and blue, a rare thing this far north. The northern lights have vanished and the previous evening feels like a dream. I breakfast on Spam, a strange tinned meat from my childhood. I'd thought that Spam had died out until I spotted a tin of it in the supermarket. I thought the wild Spam had been hunted to extinction, but some must have survived.

"People still eat this stuff?" I muttered to myself as I loaded it into my basket. "It must be fifty years since I ate this." I fancied a journey back in time.

Looking back on my childhood, it's amazing how much the British diet has changed. When I was growing up in Bebington there were two types of bread; you could have white or brown. Now the shelves of Tesco are crammed with a bewildering variety of bread. There are flatbreads, olive breads, artisan breads … Until I was around eighteen I'd never seen a pizza. Yogurt was exotic and something to be treated with caution.

Sorry if I slipped into a bit of Monty Python's Yorkshiremen sketch there. It must have been the Spam.

It's odd how you recall things differently. My nan used to fry Spam and serve it with deliciously browned chips. If I was lucky I got an egg too. This is a fondly remembered treat of my childhood. Today, on this Sutherland morning, I fry up few slices of this odd yellow meat, slip them between a sliced roll –wholemeal, of course –and wait for the ecstasy of my Nan's cooking to reappear from across the decades. It doesn't happen. The fried ham tastes bland and fatty. Perhaps my Nan cooked it better.

When I arrive back at the bridge only a few hundred yards from the road, it is a windless day. Loch Loyal stretches out before me, its surface mirror calm. I take off my pack and gaze down into the water. This small wooden bridge, connecting the isthmus that leads to Achnanclach bothy to the road, is one of my favourite places in the universe. I lean on its wooden rail and feel the sunshine on my face. I take a little time here. I rush around too much. I am often so intent on getting somewhere that I forget that simply being where I am, and taking the time to savour that moment, is of more value than always aspiring to be somewhere else. I always have to remind myself that there is an art to simply *being* somewhere. My plan had been to drive through the village of Tongue and on to one of my favourite campsites beside Loch Hope, a few miles west of where I am. The sunshine and the scent of the heather conspire with the gentle lapping of the water to slow me down.

When I reach the road it occurs to me that I need go no further, that precisely where I am would be a good place to camp. This is one of the joys of camping. You can see a spot and decide that there is no need to go further. Only a few hundred yards from where the path to the bothy begins is an old sheep pen. It is built of stone, about fifty feet across and almost perfectly round. It has one small opening where a gate must once have been. It occurs to me that inside this would be the perfect campsite, with shelter from any wind from every side. It also crosses my mind that this would also be a great defensive position if attacked by bandits. This is probably because I watched too many westerns as a child.

I have just about finished putting my tent up when dark clouds begin to scoot across the skies. By the time I am cooking my tea the temperature is beginning to fall and the tent is being shifted by a breeze that has begun to spring up. You never have to wait long for the weather to change in the Highlands. Even when I'm putting a tent up in a light breeze I know that strong gusts of wind may not be far away, so when I choose a campsite I'm always careful to find somewhere that will give me some shelter if the weather changes. Tonight's campsite, with its circular defensive wall, is well protected from any wind so I know I can relax. It's not uncommon for tents to get demolished by wind in the Highlands, even in the summer. My tipi is designed to shed wind. A bell tent is the best shape there is when it comes to windy conditions. I'm always amazed at the hot tents I see used in places like North America. These look like canvas sheds. The average Highland wind would chew them up and spit them out. Perhaps the wind doesn't blow in Canada.

One of the great joys of hot tent living is being able to cook on a wood-burning stove. You can cook "real food" and there is no need to live off tinned food, or even the dreaded dehydrated packets which tend to be the norm when you are lightweight camping. It's a joy to be able to light the stove and let that special blend of the scent of natural wood and woodsmoke permeate the air. I'm sure if you could can that odour it would beat every other air freshener there is. If I could market it, I'd call it "Lumberjack" or some other manly term. I use a heavy copper-bottom pan which I find conducts the heat of the stove very efficiently. Now that I have a damper installed in the chimney, and I have sealed the door with fire rope, I can control the stove very well and this makes cooking a lot easier. Chilli con carne is one of my outdoor favourites. It's a great feeling when the mince starts to fry on the stove, and when you add the tomatoes and chilli the smell is amazing. You could prepare such a meal with a gas stove and a heavy-duty gas cannister, but it just wouldn't be the same as one cooked over burning wood.

I'm sitting enjoying the spicy beans and mince when the disembodied voice of a woman drifts through the tent. "Is it okay if I park behind you?"

I'm a little confused as this lady has most of Sutherland to park in. I'm not sure why she would feel the need to park so close to me.

"Do you have a campervan?" I ask, wondering if the only level area they can find to park off road is behind my car.

"No, we are heading for the bothy," she tells me, with a very slight hint of a European accent.

This puzzles me even more, as the track to the bothy is a few hundred yards away and it would be much easier for her to park closer to it.

No matter to me though. "Yes, of course, no problem."

She thanks me, and I return to my meal having never set eyes on the woman. Under normal circumstances I would have at least poked my head out of the tent but the draw of the chilli is too strong and I happily return to shovelling it down my throat.

Twenty minutes later, when I'm sitting reading, I hear the voices of women chatting as they pass by my camp. One of the voices has to be the woman who asked about parking, and I realise that they are heading towards the bothy down a route that will lead them through some very difficult ground. The path they are taking will lead them to the lochside, but getting to the bridge that leads to the bothy will mean a few hundred yards of tortuous progress fighting their way through bushes, undergrowth and deep bog. Not much fun if you are carrying a rucksack full of supplies.

This time I do poke my head out of the tent and I spot three women heading for the jungle between here and the bridge. Now I have a dilemma: do I leave them to find their own route and learn the hard way, or do I call out advice and commit the ultimate sin –mansplaining? As a man of a certain age, I don't want to come across as an old man of the hills patronising these ladies but I don't want them to suffer needless exertion with their feet tangled in endless gorse bushes. Just by going to a bothy as a group of three women, they are entering what remains a male-biased domain. They are unlikely to welcome some middle-aged white man popping his bald pate out of a tent and telling them they are doing it all wrong.

I decide to risk it and call out. "There's a much easier way of getting to the bothy than that."

The women all turn in unison and glare at me –I'm done for. Then I realise they are all very relieved to hear my words and they head back up to my tent. They are festooned with equipment. Their packs have sleeping bags swinging from strings. Folding beds are strapped to their backs and their hands are full of stoves, food, pans and coal. They look more like refugees from an earthquake than bothy-goers.

A fit-looking woman in her early forties wobbles over to me with her baggage swinging. "It's our first bothy."

I may be an old git but I have the sense not to reply, *Obviously*.

Instead, I smile. "Really? It's much easier if you go down the road …"

The bag lady raises a finger to silence me. "Speak to the driver. It's no use telling me."

The driver arrives and I explain the best route to get to the bothy. She questions me thoroughly on the twists and turns of what is a very short route and it seems like she's happy to take all the mansplaining she can get. The party climb back in their car, drive the two hundred yards to where the better track begins and head off just as the light is fading.

That evening I read on the Internet that there is going to be another spectacular display of the aurora. I spend all night popping in and out of my tent, but the sky has clouded over and no Valkyries will ride this evening. I've had all the luck I am going to get.

The following morning is grey. The wind whips up the surface of the loch into white horses and the break in the weather is over. I head home to Inverness.

On Facebook I learn the identity of the three women I saw the previous day. There is even a photo of them burning the candles I left in the bothy. Their Facebook post tells of them struggling to find the bothy and arriving after dark, having discovered that it was further from the road than they expected. Perhaps my directions were not as clear as I had thought. Another Facebook bothy-goer gently mocks them for struggling to find what should be an easy bothy. I keep very quiet, remembering all the mistakes I made when I first set out to explore the bothies of the Highlands.

Chapter 22
The Monkey Puzzle Camp

I'm beginning to learn the secret of enjoying this winter, perhaps of most winters to come. It's opportunism. I watch the weather forecast avidly and try to work out which part of the Highlands is going to get the best weather. I look at wind direction and speed as a priority. The hot tent copes easily with low temperatures and I accepted long ago that it's impossible to explore the Highlands without getting rained on. It's the wind that makes the difference between an enjoyable trip and a battle with the elements. I'm increasingly realising that pitching your tent in a position to take advantage of some kind of shelter against the worst of the weather is crucial in winter. I see videos on YouTube and Facebook of intrepid wild campers setting off up hills to spend the night beneath a flimsy nylon tent with vicious winds clawing at it. The sheer noise involved must be incredible and there can be nothing relaxing about those evenings. I have spent more than a few long, sleepless nights in small lightweight tents listening apprehensively as the wind gathers itself into a ball of fury to hurl itself at my fragile shelter, trying reassure myself that the tent was going to survive. There are folk who seek out such battles with the elements and seem to enjoy them. My feeling is that, though such meteorological adventures may be exciting on the occasional night, if you are going to camp regularly they are best avoided.

In early March the forecaster tells me that Sutherland is to be raked with wild winds from the west. I turn to the islands as I've been trying to visit Mull for months, but day after day of rain filled the charts for it. At last I looked to Kinloch Hourn, a little further south and forecast to miss the worst of the weather. Kinloch Hourn is at the end of a twenty-two-mile cul-de-sac, and the last time I had been there I had promised myself I would return in the winter.

Everything always takes longer than you think. It takes me almost two and a half hours to drive from Inverness. I'm hampered by getting halfway down Loch Ness before realising I have forgotten to buy any logs for my stove. I know I have some fuel in the car and pull over to take a look in the back, hoping I have enough to get by.

My old black Skoda is a great little workhorse and never complains when I cram endless quantities of camping equipment, logs, food and furniture into it. The back of it is always chaos, and never more so than when I am setting off with my hot tent. When packing I always start out neat until I reach some mystical point where the remainder of what I have to fit in just won't quite go into the spot I had intended.

It's then that I have to get imaginative by squeezing items into the footwell of the passenger seat or wedging them into a gap next to the stout rectangular box that the stove is in. Failing that, I have to squeeze everything into the back of my hatchback and compress it in by slamming the tailgate on it before it can escape.

At campsites, some folk arrive in their cars with everything meticulously fitted into the boot. When they casually open the boot, their tent and supplies sit in neatly ordered rows. When I arrive and open the boot, an avalanche of pots and pans, tinned food, logs and underwear spills out onto the grass like children let out to play. There are advantages to having an untidy car. Since I don't exactly know what's in my car at any one time, if I need something the chances are it could be in there. If I run out of something like food or fuel, quite often a quick ferret about in the clutter of my car will produce a tin of beans or maybe corned beef hidden under a jacket, or a couple of logs wedged under the passenger seat. I could survive for a couple of weeks on the food that has slipped down into the wheel well alone.

I'm particularly fond of this campsite for a number of reasons. One of the things that attracts me is its remoteness. The Monkey Puzzle campsite sits a mile or so from the end of the Kinloch Hourn road, twenty-two miles after it leaves the A87. In the hour or so it takes me to erect my tent, no cars reach here from the narrow winding road that travels around the shore of Loch Cuaich. All around me the hills rise steeply, with great walking routes starting only yards from where I'm camping for the next few nights. The evening is still, but there are no midges this early in the year so I can enjoy a couple of hours with the tent door open, watching the changing light dancing across the water of the small loch. When the sun dips below the horizon and the shadows of the hills fall across the door of my tent, the chill of the night begins to invade. I zip the tent shut, light the stove and my lamp, and enjoy my time in glorious isolation.

The following day I set out to walk the path that heads north-east into the hills and eventually finds its way into Glen Shiel, some eleven miles and several thousand feet away. The weather is so warm I have to keep reminding myself that it is early March, and I am sweating gently as I follow the path and climb steeply beneath overhanging crags. The path is muddy at first and surrounded by saplings. There are no other footprints so this track is not often walked. A few hundred yards up the track, a gap in the trees allows me to gaze west along Loch Beag and on to where it meets the sea. The view here down this fjord-like landscape is incredible. The sea loch cuts through hills that plunge precipitously into this narrow ribbon of blue. A few hundred feet below are the white shapes of the handful of houses that constitute this tiny community. There is no phone reception here and it's about as remote as you can get while still on the mainland. The only thing that mars the view is the line of electricity pylons that march across the landscape like a procession of giant robots. Despite their presence I think the view from this spot has to be one of the finest in Scotland and it always stops me in my tracks.

I am awakened from my reveries by a croaking sound. Something moves in one of the puddles nearby and I realise it is full of mating frogs. The next mile is the same. Every pool is full of frogspawn and writhing frogs, who only break off their copulation when they sense my presence on the path. I have stumbled into the centre of a huge amphibian orgy.

For most folk the sound of the first cuckoo calling across a silent valley is the thing that tells them that spring has arrived, but not me. I always look for frogspawn in the shallow pools of the hill tracks I walk. These puddles, often no more than two inches deep and frequently less, always seem such precarious places for frogs to leave their offspring. They are always in danger of drying up under just a few days of sun. I suppose it is also true that such shallow pools also warm up quickly in the weak sun of winter. In these hills, the puddles might freeze over or be buried beneath snow. The poor frogs are threatened with habitat loss all over Britain as we drain our wetlands for building. Enough must make it through every year to ensure the survival of the species. Over this short length of track, there must be several hundred thousand tadpoles waiting to be born. If they all made it through to maturity we'd all be knee-deep in frogs.

Higher, the boggy path leads up into an empty glen. I am alone and there isn't another person in this great glen. It still surprises me that on this crowded island there are places that are seldom visited. If your aim is to find solitude it is quite possible to spend three or four days walking and see no one. This is especially true in the winter. I once spent eight days and nights in a remote bothy one winter. In all that time not one human being passed by. The only thing that I saw move was a group of four deer crossing the river one afternoon.

I am a seeker of solitude and prefer to walk alone. I develop a much closer relationship with the landscape and its nature as a solitary walker. I notice more things, seem to be able to see more and get a better sense of the place. Even walking with a close friend is a distraction, although there is a great pleasure in walking together with others and talking as you go. Thousands of people enjoy this pastime every week and walk in groups. A fair proportion of people who regularly walk in Scotland's hills would never dream of going alone. They find enjoyment in the company of others and, of course, some security. For the lone walker, a simple slip or a twisted ankle might have serious consequences and I can fully understand why many people might be cautious about hiking alone in remote places. I'm fortunate that I have never found myself in a dangerous situation while walking by myself. There have been times I have been lost, found myself wading furious rivers or twisted my ankle, but though I've often been tired and wet I've never felt at any kind of risk and I enjoy the sense of self-reliance. Perhaps the fact that I have only myself to rely on sharpens the senses.

For me, walking in the hills is an escape into another world. A place far less cluttered by the concerns we carry with us every day. If you walk with another person the rest of the world comes with you. You end up talking about politics or last night's news. It's a different experience and one I find far less valuable, but there's always the possibility that I'm just a grumpy, antisocial old man. I can't rule that out.

I wander up to the ridge and sit for a while, enjoying the cooling breeze sweeping down from the hills. I'm just about to head home when two huge shapes loom overhead. They are sea eagles, hunting carrion across the hills. Sea eagles are larger and less numerous than golden eagles. They were once extinct in the British Isles, and their reintroduction has been one of the great success stories of the limited amount of rewilding that has taken place in the UK. If the birds are far above you it can be difficult to distinguish them from the golden eagle because it is difficult to gauge their size. Sea eagles are also known as white-tailed eagles, and if you can see the white tail then you can be certain in identifying the birds. Unfortunately, the eagles only develop their white tails when they reach full maturity at around eight years old.

Even though I have seen many eagles in my time in the Scottish hills, it is a sight that never fails to excite me. Any walk that includes an eagle encounter is a day to remember. Seeing these great creatures is a privilege that is often hard-earned as normally you have to be somewhere remote to encounter them and it requires some effort to reach these places. I watch this pair of magnificent birds quartering the glen for five minutes. I am amazed by how much ground they are able to cover as they glide across hills and glens that would take me days to cover. At last they turn and sweep out of sight over one of the nearby peaks. It's only then that I can truly appreciate their size as I now realise how far away they are and how big they must be. Only sea eagles reach that kind of size.

Along with the hen harrier and red kite, they have returned from extinction to grace our skies once more. There are still folk who persecute these creatures, deliberately circulating vastly exaggerated claims that they take lambs. Some are illegally shot by a minority of sporting estates. The hen harrier is perhaps the most persecuted of all the birds of prey in Britain. Around the start of the last century it had been driven from mainland Britain, with only a few pairs remaining in the more remote Scottish islands. After legislation came in to protect the harrier it slowly re-established itself in the UK, although even now the population is largely confined to Scotland.

Back in my tent that night, I enjoy the quiet as I am alone in this glen. The only sound is the nearby stream, babbling all night long, and the occasional gust of wind that hints at a change in the weather. The following morning the sky is full of grey clouds, racing across the summits of the mountains, and the wind is sighing through the tops of a nearby group of pine trees. Rain is coming. It's time to go.

Driving back along the lochside with my tent crammed into the boot, I spot a sign beside the road. It's a shiny placard, newly erected by the estate.

It reads:

NO UNAUTHORISED VEHICLES
DOGS ON LEADS AT ALL TIMES
PLEASE KEEP TO THE PATH
NO FISHING WITHOUT A PERMIT
NO CAMPING NO FIRES

It is a sad fact that the landscape of Scotland has been shaped as much by class interests as by the wind and rain. Land ownership in the Highlands is dominated by large sporting estates, covering thousands of acres and owned by wealthy men. Most of these estates are the playthings of multimillionaires who buy an estate in Scotland in much the same way as you might buy a pair of shoes. You don't buy an estate in the Highlands to make money; you buy it because you don't need money. As a result, much of the Highlands is green desert, over-grazed by thousands of stunted deer whose populations are kept at artificially high levels. This prevents the regrowth of forestry. Huge areas are given over to grouse moors which are burnt regularly in order to keep them as open moorlands.

At long last, things are beginning to change. A new breed of landowner is emerging, mainly from overseas, who views the land differently and seeks to develop it in sympathy with the environment. The resale value of the traditional sporting estates is starting to wane as the number of people who want to have control over estates dedicated to blood sports diminishes. Despite the fact that changes are taking place, there remains a large body of landowners whose values have not altered since the Victorian era. These landowners deeply resent the intrusion of controls by government. They pay lip service to more progressive ideas, while continuing to do pretty much as they please with the land.

In Scotland, one small step forward that has made a big difference for people who enjoy the outdoors is the access legislation, which gives us the right to wander freely across our hills. In stark contrast to the England of my youth, with its legions of "Keep Out" and "Private Land" signs, in Scotland you are perfectly free to walk where you like and, importantly, to camp there for a few nights. Obviously you can't camp in someone's garden, but as long as you are sensible you can camp where you want. This is a right enshrined in law and you don't need the landowner's permission.

So, you might be wondering how the above sign came to be erected when Scotland's access legislation clearly gives you the right to walk and camp in our wild country. Here's a fictional account of what may have happened which I've written to avoid ending up in court.

~

Standing on the veranda, Lord Purdy pressed the binoculars to his eyes and felt the metal cold metal against his eye sockets. An image slowly came into focus beside the loch some half-mile from the battlements of his ancestral home as he leant against the castellated wall to steady himself.

"Good God!" the ancient aristocrat exclaimed. "It's a tent."

On the shore of the loch, he could see a green domed construction with two figures sitting outside hunched over something. Lord Purdy owned everything as far as his eyes could see, including the large expanse of water sitting half a mile from the Victorian mansion that cost huge sums of money to shore up every year. He owned the green sweeping hills he could see on the horizon and, as far as he was concerned, he owned the horizon as well.

Purdy lowered the binoculars, his face growing purple with rage. "Campbell, Campbell," he roared.

Moments later, a wooden door creaked open and a tall, greying figure hurried onto the veranda, struggling to fasten his tweed jacket. "Yes, M'lud," wheezed Campbell.

Purdy thrust the binoculars at the ageing ghillie and pointed to the shore. "What do you make of that?"

Campbell searched along the shoreline until he found the green dome. "It's campers, sir."

"I can see that. What are they doing there?" Purdy said with a snort.

Campbell searched for an explanation before noticing what might be a stove. "I think they might be cooking."

"Cooking?" Purdy struggled with the notion for a moment.

"Yes, sir. Baked beans maybe, or sausages."

Understanding flickered in Purdy's eyes. "Like the Famous Five stories Nanny used to read to me, you mean. 'Jolly fine grub' and all that?"

"Exactly, sir," Campbell stammered.

"Well, go and tell them to bugger off. They can go and explore some other rural idyll somewhere else," announced Purdy, like a judge pronouncing a sentence.

Campbell hesitated, running his fingers through his grey hair. He framed his words carefully. "I can't, sir."

Purdy's eyes widened. "It's my land –tell them go to hell. Take the dogs if you want."

Campbell looked down, knowing he was about to deliver bad news. "Sir, it's … They've got a right to be there."

Purdy snatched back the binoculars. "They have a right to be on my land?"

"Yes, sir. That access legislation they brought in."

Purdy glared through the binoculars as if he was trying to move the tent by the force of his stare alone. "Oh, I heard about that nonsense. Bloody government and their meddling laws. Can't kill this, can't kill that."

Campbell nodded vigorously. "What do they know, M'lud?"

Purdy's brow furrowed as he brooded, deep in thought. "What's the point of having the countryside if you can't slaughter everything that's in it? Tell me that."

Campbell peered over at the campers. "They're probably some of those vegetarians."

"Vegans, more like." The two men shared a brief shudder of disgust. "Eating that damned couscous rubbish they're so fond of."

Campbell shook his head sadly. "What is couscous, sir?"

Purdy snorted. "Damned if I know."

A gust of wind tore across from the water's edge, ruffling the Purdy standard as it passed.

Glancing up, Purdy watched as the wind animated the flag. It bore the crest of a lord beating a peasant with a stick. "Can't we just ignore the law, like we normally do?"

Campbell shook his head sadly. "Afraid not, sir."

Purdy fell silent and paced the battlements for a few

moments before turning in triumph. "A sign's what we need."

Campbell shuffled. "A sign, sir?"

"Yes. 'KEEP OFF. NO CAMPING.' That sort of thing." Purdy grinned in triumph.

"But that's illegal," Campbell stammered, his eyes wide with alarm.

Purdy shrugged. "Well, technically, I suppose –but most of these bloody fool campers won't know that, will they?"

Campbell brightened as he grasped the idea. "I suppose they won't, sir. I'll get on to it right away."

Minutes later, alone on the battlements, Lord Purdy lit a large cigar and watched as the smoke curled into the air. "They won't know it's illegal," he chuckled. "And besides, if they do work out it's illegal, I didn't put that sign up. It was that damn fool, Campbell. How was I supposed to know?"

~

The bottom line is that if you see a "NO CAMPING" sign in Scotland, you can ignore it. The only exception to this is places where you would normally pay for access, like castle grounds and gardens. Oddly it also means that you can't camp on a campsite if it's closed. This led to a bizarre situation during Covid-19 restrictions: when the campsite at Loch Morlich closed, it became the one place you couldn't camp in the Cairngorm National Park. This was doubly ironic since, in a roundabout way, that campsite is on ground that is publicly owned. I didn't make that bit up, I promise.

The road back to the A87 is a long winding single track,

typical of many in the Highlands. This road is made all the more interesting by the fact that, for long sections, it cuts through thickly wooded areas which means it's impossible to see what is coming round the next corner. This can lead to surprises. As I go round a bend, I meet a four-wheel drive vehicle coming the other way –except it's not coming. It has driven almost completely off the road and is tottering precariously at forty-five degrees, threatening to turn over at any moment. Fortunately, the folk in it have all climbed out safely and are standing around wondering what to do.

As I step out of the car, a large bald man with a Birmingham accent approaches me, looking hopeful. "Are you a local?"

"Er, sorry, no," I tell him.

His face falls, but he still seems to think I must be some sort of expert on single-track roads. "Do you think we can drive it out of here?"

I try to look knowledgeable. "Well, it's not damaged now but if it rolls it'll get a lot of damage, so I'd get it towed out."

Everyone seems to think this is a good idea so, as there's no phone signal, I give the man a lift to the estate office a mile or so down the road where he will be able to arrange to get his vehicle pulled out.

"I was looking at the scenery," he tells me, trying to explain how he managed to drive off an empty road.

If you are not familiar with single-track roads in the Highlands, it might be helpful for me to explain a few things. There are still a lot of roads in the Highlands where two cars cannot pass. These roads are widened every now and again to allow cars travelling in the opposite directions to get by each other. Single-track roads are tricky things. They are often through incredibly beautiful scenery, constantly luring your gaze upwards to take in the view. This is a trap. These roads are, by definition, narrow. The margin for error when driving along them is small. Just as my friend from Birmingham found, a moment's inattention can put you in a ditch, or much worse –like the time I spoke of earlier in this series when I screeched to a halt, inches from the grille of a lorry on a remote and empty single-track road in Sutherland. We had both been looking at the view.

Tip Number 1

No matter how tempting it is to let your eyes wander, keep them glued to the tarmac. Not only are these roads narrow but they are also prone to dart off in unexpected directions with absolutely no warning. You won't find any warning signs for bends on these roads because the whole road is composed of bends. It would make more sense to signpost a straight section.

Tip Number 2

Pay close attention to the location of the next passing place. I am terrible at reversing. I've been driving for over forty years, yet I am still prone to reverse into a ditch whenever I attempt to go backwards, so I do everything I can to avoid that. My strategy is that if I can only see one passing place, I try to make sure I get there first before anyone can pass it and force me to reverse.

Tip Number 3

Know the rules for using a single-track road. There is a complicated set of ethics for using a single-track road and it helps to know these even if you don't always follow them. If you meet another driver head on, the one closest to the nearest passing place should reverse into it. Unless one of you is driving a much larger vehicle which is difficult to reverse, in which case the smaller vehicle has to back up, or unless you are on a steep hill, in which case the driver coming uphill has right of way. Simple, isn't it?

Tip Number 4

Pull in to let faster vehicles overtake. This is, without doubt, the rule that causes the greatest frustration and friction between local drivers, who are trying to get somewhere quickly, and tourists, who are cruising along enjoying the view. I've lost count of the number of times I've been part of a crocodile of furious drivers sitting steaming in their cars behind a big white campervan that rarely gets above twenty miles an hour but never lets anyone pass. It's almost always a pensioner who spent his lump sum on a gigantic campervan and then drives it around the narrowest roads he can find and never, and I mean never, uses his rear-view mirror. Before you rise up in defence of pensioners, I should point out that I am one so I am perfectly entitled to criticise my fellow crumblies.

Campervans used to be seasonal visitors to the Highlands, migrating south when the winter came. Now I am starting to see them all year round. Probably another effect of climate change.

Chapter 23
Gunter's Leg

The leg lies on the bare bothy table, cold, hard and lifeless. I test the knife against my hand. It's sharp, but is it sharp enough? Gunter's leg is very tough. I've tried stabbing it a few times and barely made an impression –it is almost fossilised. The thought of eating it turns my stomach but I had promised, and it was very important to Gunter. No matter how I feel about it, I know how disappointed he'd be if I didn't eat it so I try to quell my heaving stomach, take the knife and begin to cut.

⁓

The Ardtornish estate sits on the western fringe of the Ardnamurchan peninsula, and on this Friday afternoon it is being deluged by rain. I know this because I am in one of their bothies, watching rivulets of water running down the window. The rain batters against the window panes, the old bothy windows trembling with its impact. The windows have withstood countless storms like this one but they can't last forever, and when the hardest squalls come in I worry they'll give in to the deluge and shatter at my feet. I have to remember the bucket upstairs, catching the constant drip from a broken ceiling light. Every twenty minutes or so I have to go up the stairs and empty it.

Staring through the rain-spattered glass, I follow the track to where it vanishes behind the dark shape of the old ruined cottage. That is the spot where the colonel should be appearing about now, together with our bothy guest, Gunter. It was the Colonel who invited Gunter. I've never met Gunter, an old Austrian translator, but the colonel bumped into him in Kervaig, the remote white-walled bothy that sits on the northern edge of Scotland, dipping its toes in the Atlantic. The colonel and I have known each other or a couple of years now and have exclusive use of this isolated bothy in western Scotland.

Some of you will remember that the colonel, of course, isn't a real army officer. His name is Peter, but his military bearing and fondness for dressing in ex-military outdoor equipment have earnt him that nickname amongst the bothy fraternity. It had taken the colonel some time to persuade me to come this weekend. Having seen the weather forecast, I was reluctant to head west this weekend as I didn't want a soaking. On the walk in to the bothy yesterday, I had been lucky. The rain had held off as I followed the path beside the river up through the oak woods. The trees had dripped water, and mist had hung in the air, but I avoided the expected soaking until I emerged into open country where the glen widens and

I crossed the open glen, at the start of the last mile to the bothy. Here the ground becomes increasingly boggy. I have been here many times and know the route intimately, which is just as well as some patches of bog are much deeper than others, threatening to swallow the unwary traveller. I made it across the rickety bridge that is the shaky gateway to the bothy before the first heavy drops of rain fell, heralding a solid downpour that had lasted all night and all of this day.

Peter had phoned me and told me he had invited Gunter who had been keen to spend time writing his next book in the remote bothy. Gunter moved to London some years ago from his home in Europe and had told our mutual friend that he found it hard to concentrate with the hubbub of the metropolis around him. Ever helpful, Peter had suggested he come to our little haven and spend a week or so working on his novel. Gunter was keen and the colonel persuaded me that the two of us could settle our guest into the bothy and then leave him to his creative quest. So here I am, watching through the window for Gunter and the colonel to arrive on the track to the bothy as it emerges from the bog and passes the dark stone of the ruined cottage.

I expected them an hour ago and had lit the tall cast iron stove to warm the bothy, but they still had not appeared on the rain-washed track. Perhaps Gunter's train had been delayed or they had needed to stop off in Fort William to buy some supplies. Tired of watching at the window, I settle down with one of the many bird books on the bothy's bookshelf and attempt to busy myself trying to memorise the bird species that occupy this rich habitat. I have tried this before and ended up frustrated as I forget the identities of birds at about the same rate I am able to learn them.

After twenty minutes I glance up and spot movement by the ruin some half-mile away. A tall figure, swathed in camouflage waterproofs and carrying a massive rucksack, is striding down the path. Strangely he is alone. There is no mistaking the colonel, but where is Gunter? The rain refuses to abate and when a ferocious squall sweeps in moments later I lose sight of my friend. He'll be wet and cold no doubt. I throw some more coal on the fire and head into the frigid kitchen to put the kettle on for the obligatory reviving cup of tea.

Ten minutes later the colonel stands before me, his Soviet special forces survival waterproofs dripping pools of rain water onto the floor.

"Where's Gunter?" I ask, as I place the steaming pot of tea on the ancient bothy table.

"Oh Gawd," the colonel responds, dropping his 1947 Prussian paratrooper's rucksack onto the floor with a thud that rattles the windows.

The colonel has never been one to leave something behind. He shuns anything that could be described as lightweight, preferring things that were manufactured with the express aim of surviving sustained shelling over anything that might be described as lightweight. His cooking stove is solid brass, and if you were to throw it at an oncoming tank it would stop it dead. I can see he is troubled but wait until he is ready to tell me what has happened.

He shakes a small ocean from his waterproof jacket and looks at me sadly. "It's taken me two hours to get him up the track."

"That's twice the usual time." I peer out of the window but there is no sign of the Austrian. "Where is he?"

"He told me he was holding me up. Insisted I go on," the colonel tells me, shaking his head sadly. "And he's given us this."

The colonel heaves his rucksack across the floor and I notice that there is a package about four feet long strapped to the back. It is wrapped in black plastic to keep the rain out, and is rifle-shaped with a bulge at one end.

"What the hell is it?" I say, picking it up. It is surprisingly heavy.

The colonel shrugs. "Special present he said, for the boys in the bothy."

We sit in silence drinking tea, glancing out of the window and waiting for Gunter to appear. He doesn't.

I've never met Gunter and am curious. "How old is this guy?"

"Seventy, maybe. It's hard to say."

"And you met him at Kervaig bothy?"

The colonel nods, looking a little embarrassed. "I thought he was fit. Well, he got to Kervaig."

"You can get a bus almost to Kerviag," I point out, recalling the ramshackle minibus that carries passengers the eleven miles from where the ferry lands to the lighthouse at

Cape Wrath, passing close to the bothy as it does so.

"Yes, I hadn't thought of that." The colonel springs to his feet. "He should be here by now."

I peer out through the rain which is growing in intensity. "I can't see any sign of him."

"Right." One thing you can say about the colonel is that he is decisive.

Moments later, he and I are swathed in waterproofs and making our way gingerly across the bridge in search of the Austrian author. The bog is deepening rapidly as the rain cascades down, torrents running down from the surrounding hills. Daylight is also fading and I can see the colonel is worried for his guest. He break into a run past the ruined cottage. The rain is blinding both of us but I catch a glimpse of movement out in the bog.

"There!" I point into the curtain of rain.

"Oh, thank god." We run towards the half-sunken figure of Gunter, zigzagging to avoid the deepest pools.

He is wedged up to his waist in the mire. He looks older than seventy, but very few of us look our best after we've been immersed in a Highland bog and rained on for several hours so I give him the benefit of the doubt.

I carry his rucksack and the Colonel half carries, half drags Gunter the rest of the way to the bothy. All the while he protests that he is perfectly fine and doesn't need our help. Despite his protestations, he has a bad limp.

He collapses when crossing a deep pool, yelling out in anger. "Damn this leg. It always lets me down."

The colonel lifts him gently out of the muddy pool. "Are you alright, old chap?"

By now, Gunter looks about ninety as he tries to shrug off the colonel's support. "I'd be better off without this leg. Leave me alone."

The protestations cease when we reach the bridge. His eyes widen in terror when he sees what he has to cross. It is a daunting sight. The little causeway could never be described as a great feat of engineering. It consists of three large tree trunks spanning some thirty feet of Highland burn. At one time these logs had been joined by planks nailed across all three, which must have made a passable walkway. That time is now long gone –as is one of the tree trunks. All that remains now are two tree trunks, one of which is almost cracked in half, and a series of rotten planks clinging to the bridge with gaps looking like the smile of a geriatric tramp.

During dry periods the stream, or burn as it's called in the Highlands, is often reduced to a mere trickle. After the rain over the last few days it is raging down the glen, a dark rolling monster which roars and carries off everything before it. Falling in the river now would be to plunge into a life-and-death struggle. To get to the bothy, the only way is to cross what remains of the bridge.

Gunter is terrified by the prospect. "I will go home."

This alarms the colonel. "You need to get dry, old chap. Can't have you attempting that bog again. You can hang on to me."

Gunter doesn't look too enthusiastic about the idea but

seems to realise there's no other option. He has to face the bridge or the bog, and both are formidable opponents right now.

The colonel is around six feet two inches. Gunter is about a foot shorter. Gingerly, he grabs the colonel's camouflage webbing belt and the pair sets off across the bridge. Normally we adopt the rule of only one person at a time on the flimsy bridge, but now there is no option but for the two to cross together. The bridge sags alarmingly under their combined weight. I decide that this is not the time to point out the structural inadequacy of the bridge and remain silent as the pair shuffle over.

At last they step onto the grassy bank at the far side of the raging burn and minutes later we are all standing dripping in the shelter of the bothy.

"I am wet," Gunter announces, and begins to take off his sodden clothes.

This is the first time I've been able to get a close look at our guest. His long grey hair is plastered to his face. He is short and rather plump. His cagoule looks about thirty years old and has numerous holes in it. His jacket looks like it put up only token resistance to the rain and surrendered to the attack hours ago.

"You are soaked," I state needlessly, as I hand him his rucksack.

He's down to his string vest now. "It's okay, I have spare clothes."

He does have spare clothes in his rucksack. All are packed in plastic bags. All are cotton. The plastic bags have more holes in them than his cagoule, so all his spare clothes are soaked.

He looks at them disconsolately while the colonel heads off to put the kettle on. I offer him some of my dry clothes. I keep a stock of them in the bothy for just such an occasion, but he refuses and sits down beside the stove in his threadbare white underwear.

I head into the kitchen and whisper to the Colonel as he puts teabags in the teapot. "He won't get dressed."

The Colonel shrugs. "I couldn't do anything with him on the way up the track, old chap. Wouldn't listen to a word. He's a stubborn old bird."

"He's sitting by the stove in his vest. You know what that is, don't you?" I ask.

The colonel looks puzzled.

I gather some mugs together. "That's paradoxical undressing. Sure sign of exposure. We better get some tea in him quick."

The Colonel looks alarmed. "He's not going to die on us, is he?"

We get some tea in him but only after he insists that we add another three teabags to the pot to make a brew that would take the paint off the woodwork. Despite both our remonstrations, he still refuses to get dressed. I do the only thing I can and stock the old stove as though I am trying to get the Flying Scotsman up to speed. We spend the night with Gunter shivering by the stove, surrounded by his steaming clothes, while the colonel and I gently sweat in our very own bothy sauna. After two hours of this, colour begins to return to his cheeks and the Colonel and I have lost a stone and a half between us.

By morning Gunter has revived a little although he's still only able to wobble unsteadily around the bothy. The rain has stopped and I can relax as it looks like nobody is going to die immediately. By this point, our guest has decided that bothy life is not for him and insists he is leaving.

He sits drinking the foul brew he describes as tea. He has brought some of his own tea leaves which infuse his brew until it turns the colour of creosote. He refuses to take any food, insisting he will walk out that day.

The Colonel had wanted to spend another night in the bothy but is adamant that Gunter shouldn't walk out alone. I had planned on a longer stay and am happy to spend another couple of days there, so I watch the pair pack. At least Gunter has dry clothes now.

Just before leaving, Gunter summons both of us to the lounge and draws himself up to his full height of five feet four inches.

"And now," he announces, like the master of ceremonies at a civic function, "I give you my leg to eat."

The Colonel is speechless. I manage a, "Sorry?"

"Here it is—" and Gunter produces the parcel that the colonel carried in the previous evening. We had forgotten about it in the panic to revive our patient.

We watch as he takes a knife and cuts through the black plastic. What emerges from the wrapping is a leg of some kind. The nearest animal I can think of is a dinosaur.

Gunter swells with pride. "Finest ham from my country."

"Where's he from?" I whisper to the colonel.

The colonel thinks for a second. "Wolverhampton?"

Gunter hands the leg to me ceremoniously and I take it like a celebrity receiving a bouquet. It is hard and yellow and looks like it may have been preserved in a peat bog for a very long time. I look at it, puzzled.

"Eat and enjoy," Gunter says, before noticing the look of horror in my eyes. "It's very good," he adds, sounding a little hurt.

The colonel has shrunk down into his army fatigues, as if he hopes the camouflage will render him invisible.

I try to smile back, not wanting to hurt Gunter's feelings. "Yes, I'm sure it is. We will enjoy it."

Gunter looks at me intently, obviously not believing I have any intention of eating the leg which, of course, I don't. "You promise you'll eat it now. Very delicious."

"Yes, of course, I promise. Looks … very nice." I carry my prize into the kitchen and set it down on the table.

The colonel follows me in and looks at the leg suspiciously. "It's pretty solid. I don't fancy your chances with that, old chap."

I have no intention of tackling the thing alone. "What do you mean, my chances? It's for you as well."

The colonel shakes his head. "Me? No, very sorry. Strict vegetarian."

"You are not," I hiss. "What about that bacon the other weekend?"

He looks a little embarrassed. "Minor lapse, that."

"And the beef the other weekend?"

He raises his hand as if taking a vow. "I have sworn to my Missus. No more meat shall pass my lips. Besides, it was you that promised."

I don't believe a word. Faced with the prospect of eating Gunter's leg I would happily swear off eating meat for the rest of my life, but I doubt that the colonel has done so. One part of what he said is true, though –I have promised.

Later that morning, I help the colonel get Gunter across the bridge and then follow their progress up the track until they vanish behind the ruin. I resolve to have a word with the colonel. Next time we invite someone to our retreat in the hills we'll have to be certain that they are capable of getting themselves in –and more importantly, out –under their own steam. Gunter had come close to having a serious incident and that is something we need to avoid in future.

I settle down to read my bird book but I can't concentrate. I know that the leg is lying in the kitchen, waiting for me. I have always prided myself on my hearty appetite, and shortly before noon my stomach begins its customary communications, telling me that now is the time to begin looking for lunch. My stomach doesn't know about the leg.

I am not a fussy eater. I never bother about sell-by dates or any of that nonsense. I'll eat pretty much anything. So why not Gunter's leg?

It lies on the kitchen table, pale, mute and solid. Daring me to eat it.

"Now, come on. Man up. How bad can it be?" I ask myself.

I find the sharpest knife we had, an antique bone-handled affair, and approach the leg. It looks even less appetising than it did before, if that is possible. Old episodes of *Silent Witness* flash through my mind, the ones where she talks in that clinical voice: "We have the severed leg of some sort of animal. Species unknown. I am making the first incision," she would say, as she raises the scalpel.

All I have is a worn-out kitchen knife. I slice through the plastic outer coating and then saw off as thin a sliver of meat as I can. An image of a priest carving up the severed leg of a saint flashes into my mind. I push it away.

"Don't be stupid. Just carve a bit off and eat it." There's a lot of this leg and it occurs to me I could be eating this thing for a long time.

I put the slice of meat between two slices of bread. Think of England. I shove it in my mouth and start to chew. The meat is tough. I keep chewing. The meat doesn't yield. I chew further. Soon the bread has gone but the meat is just sitting in my mouth. I chew on. My jaw begins to ache. I keep chewing. Then it feels as if my teeth are starting to loosen. Never mind, I'm made of stern stuff.

"This thing won't beat me," I mutter, still chewing.

Then it does beat me. I can't chew anymore. I spit out the flesh –it's unmarked. I've made no impression on it. I would have more chance of eating the soles of my boots. I realise all attempts at consuming this gift were futile. Rubbing my aching jaw muscles, I try to come up with a plan. I've done my best but what am I going to do with it now?

"I could bury it," I suggest, talking to myself as no one else is here, but I don't like the idea of it lying outside the bothy in some shallow grave.

"I could burn it." But in order to burn it, I'd need to saw it up so I could fit in the stove and then I'd have to spend the night listening to it sizzling. That would be an uncomfortable sound to have to listen to in the quiet of the bothy. Even if it would burn, which I doubt, what about the smell? Something reminds me of Robert Service's poem, *The Cremation of Sam McGee*, when the prospector begins to dread the corpse in the flames. I shiver at the thought. I'll not burn it then. I decide I'll have to carry it back out of the bothy. That's the only thing for it.

That evening, as I sit in the bothy warming myself beside the stove in the candlelight, I begin to feel increasingly uneasy about the lump of flesh lying on the table like some macabre relic from an autopsy. I am not by nature a superstitious man. I have slept in many supposedly haunted bothies and my slumbers have never been disturbed. I've heard lots of creaks, groans and rattles a long way from any other human being and have never felt the slightest unease. Yet tonight, the thing in the kitchen next door occupies my mind in an increasingly unhealthy way.

Then it occurs to me. "I'll put it outside. Maybe something will take it away."

I realise immediately that the idea of anything in the Scottish countryside taking that lump of meat away is ridiculous.

Gunter's leg weighs over six kilograms and is rock solid. No fox could carry it away. The only animal I can think of that might be able to make an impression on it is a badger. Even then, I am certain that a badger won't be able to carry it off and would have to resort to gnawing away at it. Nevertheless, I decide I'll be happier if the damn thing is out of the bothy.

The night is dark and the air filled with a fine drizzle as I carry the leg a few hundred yards from the bothy and hurl it onto a small mound. Once the leg is gone, I can relax. It will be there in the morning and I can carry it out. That would be the end of Gunter's leg and I would be glad to see the back of it. I spend the night quietly sipping my whisky and watching the fire, eventually turning in at around 10:00 p.m.

I sleep soundly, perhaps happy in the knowledge that I am legless in the bothy. It must be around 2:00 a.m. when my bladder decides it is full and insists I get up. Reluctantly I grope for my head torch, climb out of my sleeping bag and totter down the bothy stairs to use the facilities outside.

The drizzle of the early evening has cleared and now the Moon peers down onto the glen from above the dark outline of the surrounding ridges. I watch a shooting star cut across the sky as I relieve myself. Then, and I don't know what makes me do this, I decide I will check on the leg. I stroll a few yards over to where I had left it sitting on the small mound. To my amazement, it is no longer there. Something has taken it. I search the grass around the mound to be certain but there is no sign of it.

Something powerful has carried it off. The realisation that

there is an animal capable of doing that out here in the dark glen sends a shiver down my spine. Suddenly I feel very alone and a long way from the bothy. I cast my torch about in a great arc, just to check there is nothing close, then freeze in terror. There, a few hundred yards away and on the other side of the rickety bridge, I can see a pair of eyes reflected in my torch beam. Something is watching me. I run for the bothy. Back inside, I secure the bolts and lean against the door, breathing heavily.

I still spend as much time in bothies alone as I always did. I have rationalised that the chances of being attacked by anything are small. Only one thing has changed. These days, when I go out at night, I never look at the stars. I keep my torch scanning the hillside, just in case the creature that ate Gunter's leg is somewhere out there in the darkness.

Chapter 24
The Wild Isle

There are some places that call me back over and over again. These are places I form an intimate connection with, places that speak to my inner voice.

"I must spend more time here," I think. "I will come back here again."

These may be particular bothies or hills, perhaps the side of a loch or a riverbank. These are special places on Earth where I feel at ease. Everyone has these places and probably makes the same sort of promises I do, but somehow life seems to get in the way. A million small things trip us up and take away our attention. I've always got something else to do and swear that once that's done I'll go somewhere special. I haven't yet learnt to ignore those things and go to my special places instead.

One such place for me is the Isle of Mull. I've been there a handful of times and each time I promise to return. I always find that I've left it longer than I thought, yet with each visit the urge to return grows. The Scottish islands are great places to explore in a hot tent. If you have never visited them it is important to realise the scale of these places. Many of the Scottish islands are huge. The Western Isles, or Outer Hebrides, is an archipelago that stretches for over one hundred miles. The islands are linked by ferries but it is difficult to travel the full length of the Westerns Isles in a single day due to the need to get the sequence of ferries right. To the north, the Orkney and Shetland Isles again have a very different character, with these islands steeped in the Norse culture of the Vikings.

There are many opportunities for wild camping in the islands, as their populations are frequently sparse and there are many open spaces that a camper can use. The remoteness of these islands and the need for those who live on them to be self-sufficient has led to an understanding attitude towards folk who like to live unrestricted lives. If you visit the remoter Scottish islands, it is worth remembering that these are places where the simplest thing –obtaining a spare part for a vehicle, for example –can take three or four times longer than it would on the mainland. Those who live here are accustomed to such timescales and accept them as a part of island life. If you visit the Scottish islands, it helps to not be in a hurry.

Mull has a richly deserved reputation as one of the best places to see wildlife in Scotland. The air is populated by a thriving population of sea eagles and many other native birds. The seas around the island have large numbers of dolphins and minke whales. Driving along the roads of the island, you will see signs indicating the crossing places of otters and asking you to slow down. Exploring the island is the task of years rather than months. There are three hundred miles of coastline and the island has an area of three hundred and thirty eight square miles. Those dry facts don't convey just how vibrant a place Mull is. My eyes are never far off the weather forecast and, in mid-April, the forecast suggests there are to be a few days of exceptionally fine weather. I pack my tent into my car and set off, deciding to call in to the bothy on the Ardtornish estate where Gunter's leg vanished as it's on the way and will make a good stopping-off point on the way to the Mull ferry.

There was a time I came to this bothy at least once every month. I used it to write some of my books. If you want to get serious about writing there is no better way than to take yourself somewhere where there is no TV, no Internet and no phone connection, and your nearest neighbour is three miles away. You write because you have to; there is nothing else to do anyway. My record in this bothy is a nine-day stretch one bleak December. Apart from one visit to the nearest village, Lochaline, to resupply, I saw no one for the whole time. Once a day I would climb the hill behind the bothy to the point where I could get a phone signal, just to check the rest of the world was doing okay without me. It turned out the world managed just fine and I got a lot of my book written. Writing a book is like pushing a great big boulder up a hill. It takes time and it always feels like a long way. As long as that boulder is moving, your book is getting written. If it stops moving because you have stopped writing then the book is in limbo.

You feel as if you are getting nowhere and the boulder starts to feel really heavy. It gets to the stage you think you just can't push any further just before you suddenly reach the top of the hill and the boulder rolls away.

For this reason I know this bothy well. On this visit, I know that it is at least three months since anyone was here and those people were me, the Colonel and Gunter, plus his leg. The old wooden door swings open and I step into a timeless place. The dark corridor has known only silence for endless days. Weeks have come and gone, months have passed, and all has been still as if the place was frozen by an enchanted spell. The mug I washed three months ago sits upended on the draining board. The candles by the stove have been dark and dead since I blew them out. I run my hand across the surface of the table where I sat for hours writing my last book. Strangely there is no dust. I realise that for dust to fall on a surface, you need movement to create the tiny currents of air that deposit these specks of existence. Nothing has moved here so there is no dust. Time was still and I have broken the silence.

It's late by the time I arrive and it will be dark in less than an hour. I have one thing to do before I move into my familiar routine of fire-lighting and cooking my evening meal. There is one visit I must make.

I step out into the cooling air of the day as the shadows lengthen across the glen. There is no wind, and the only sound apart from my footsteps is of water trickling from the low burn. I walk around the back of the bothy and examine the base of the rear wall. Here, I am delighted to see a number of small bundles of fur and bones. These are owl pellets. They tell me that there is still an owl in residence in the nest box above the derelict stable beside the bothy. Two years ago, or maybe more, the colonel and I hauled the owl box I had made up the track in a small cart. It was July and the glen was oppressively hot that day. By the time we reached the bothy, both of us were exhausted and soaked in sweat, not to mention bad-tempered having been bled dry by the huge numbers of clegs (horsefly) that had bred that year. There were no midges because of the heat. Midges don't like it sunny. When the midges head home for their afternoon siesta, they give the clegs a shout. After all, it would never do if two men were allowed to walk through a Highland glen and not lose a token amount of blood to the local populace.

I'd found the plans for the box on the Barn Owl Trust website. A barn owl is a fairly large bird so the box has to be pretty substantial to accommodate both parents and, hopefully, owlets. It also needs to have a small balcony beneath the entrance so that young birds can get exercise and learn to fly. As a result, it was a lot heavier than I had anticipated and shifting it three miles by manpower was no mean feat.

I wanted to install the box because when we first visited the bothy, after it had lain unused for years, we had found the body of a barn owl inside. It had found its way in through a broken window but had been unable to find its way back out and so had starved to death. A sad end to such a beautiful bird. My ambition was to bring a barn owl back to the bothy. For the first two years, the box lay unused. Perhaps I had done something wrong, like set it in the wrong place for example.

I phoned the Barn Owl trust and asked them why my box might be lying unused.

"You have to remember barn owls don't look for nest boxes. They look for holes," the advisor explained.

Perhaps the open-ended roof space wasn't offering the small holes that owls look for. I realised the situation of the box, in the roof space of the old stable, would mean that it would be a pretty cold place when the wind blew through, as there were open spaces at either end. One afternoon, after the box had been lying empty for two years, I boarded over one end of the barn, leaving only a small section that an owl could get through. Perhaps if an owl was attracted by the gap it might enter the roof space and see the box. Other than fitting a vole dispenser in there, I couldn't think of any other way to make it more attractive. I knew there were barn owls about three miles away and as they are territorial animals, young birds would have to be searching for nest spaces in our area. Since the bothy was the only structure for miles that could offer the kind of accommodation they would be looking for, we had to be in with a chance of getting a tenant.

I visited the bothy again about eighteen months before my current visit and found, to my delight, that there were owl pellets near the bothy. I climbed the ladder into the roof space, my legs trembling with excitement, and peered in. There was straw nesting material clearly visible. The box had a resident. I was incredibly pleased and filled with a real sense of achievement. I felt I had restored something. I had built the box with my own hands, hauled it in to the bothy and erected it. Most of my time I am sitting in front of a keyboard when I make something, so it feels good to have handled the wood and screwed it all together. Sometimes it's nice to make something you can touch. I also took satisfaction in knowing that perhaps barn owls will live in the box for years to come. It felt as much an achievement as any of the books I have written.

Knowing the owl is there and seeing it are two different things. I have managed to get a very brief image of the bird on my camera trap, so I know that I am not mistaken and it really is a barn owl. I have sat by the window of the bothy at dusk and daybreak but not caught sight of the barn owl that lives next door. Wildlife is like that: it never turns up when you expect. I'll see the owl when I'm not looking for it. One day I'll be going to collect water or emptying the ashes from the fire and the bird will casually fly past. It would be typical of my luck if I was knocked off the fragile bridge to the bothy by a careless barn owl and drowned.

The following day I say goodbye to the bothy and head for the ferry terminal in the tiny village of Lochaline. The Highland village is typical of so many on the west coast of Scotland. It has a shop and a pub and a small cluster of houses. Central to its existence is the concrete slipway that leads down to the sea where the ferry docks. My first visit to Mull must have been thirty years ago when I made the journey with members of the Inverness Mountaineering Club. We were sitting on Lochaline slipway waiting for the ferry when our driver, Ian, a veteran club member, announced he was going to get himself a KitKat from the little kiosk in the car park. I was in the back of the car with Helen, a woman who was new to the club. Helen was a born-again Christian and seemed to look down on the rest of us in the club as we were rather uncouth and prone to swearing and beer drinking. Despite Helen's very different attitude to life, we did our best to accommodate her and tried to moderate our language when she was in earshot.

Ian stepped out of the car and headed for the little shop. As he did so, the car began to gradually roll forward. In his haste to get chocolate, Ian had forgotten to apply the handbrake. The car gathered speed and the sea, at the end of the slipway, approached at an alarming rate. At this point Helen, conscious of her own mortality, let out a stream of expletives that would have embarrassed a Liverpool docker. One can only hope the Lord was otherwise engaged at the time. I leant forward, jerked the handbrake on and the car stopped. We sat in silence waiting for Ian to return. When he did, I remarked how lovely the primroses had been that year.

Now, thirty years later, I sit waiting for the ferry on that same slipway. The ferry is painted in the customary black and white livery of Caledonian MacBrayne, the company that runs most of the ferries that connect the Scottish islands. These ferries make life on the islands possible as they bring all the people, vehicles and supplies across. The coming and going of these ferries dictates the rhythm of island life for thousands of people. If you are travelling anywhere or meeting guests then you have to work with the ferry timetable. Their importance to islanders can't be overestimated.

On that visit we camped on the shores of Loch na Keal, a big sea loch that cuts into the island from the west. I remembered the flat grasslands that run between the road and the shoreline from that trip thirty years ago. Back then we had climbed Ben More, the highest hill on Mull. Ben More is just a little over 3,00 feet high. The mountain dips its toes in the sea and to ascend it you start at sea level so, unlike many other Scottish hills, you have to climb its entire height to make it to the top.

I'll climb the hill tomorrow. Today I'll make my camp on the extensive area of flat grass between the single-track road and the sea. I pitch the tent in warm sun and a gentle breeze. The weather is so warm that I'm finding it hard to believe this is still April and we have yet to pass Easter. My memories of this place are accurate: it is a near-ideal wild campsite. The sea is glittering blue and behind me the hills rise, their green grassy flanks dotted white with sheep. A mile or so away, across the inlet, the shore is dotted with the white outlines of cottages and the occasional larger house. There is a feeling of space, and here Mull has that timeless quality of many Scottish islands. The view I am looking at has changed very little in the last two hundred years. In common with many areas of the Highlands the population of Mull has declined over the last few hundred years. The population is now more or less stable at around three thousand folk, which has reduced over the last few centuries from a height of around ten thousand.

The camping is ideal for a hot tent as it is possible to camp all along the single-track road that follows the sea. The grassed area sits on top of the shingle beach and so it is well drained and nowhere is it boggy. You can find information about this camping area in the last chapter, where I list a few good campsites.

Mull is a reasonably accessible island as a ferry sails here from the small port of Oban, around an hour north of Glasgow. It can be fairly busy in the summer, although "busy" is a relative term and I suspect that if you are used to the traffic jams of the Lake District or the hordes of Snowdonia, you will find Mull quiet even at the height of the tourist season. If you look around you are almost certain to find a quiet spot. As is almost always the case in the Highlands, if you walk a mile from the road, you will see no one.

After a quiet night at my campsite with only sheep for company, I drive three miles along the coast road to where the path up Ben More begins. For April the place is busy, although it is a Sunday and the weather is incredible for the time of year. It's warm and sunny, and today would be classed as good weather for a June day. The truth is that this weather is unnaturally good. It's the warmest weather I have ever seen this early in the year. Climbing Ben More at this time of year, I should be encased in waterproofs, battling through squalls of rain and hail. Yet here I am puffing my way up the hill, sweating gently, in a tee shirt and light trousers.

Even though the weather has been very dry over the last few months, the first mile of the climb is boggy. The mountain grows steadily steeper the higher I climb. It is the curse of the ageing hill walker to find the fact that age has slowed you being emphasised by every passing walker. Many years ago, when I was young, fit and lean, no one ever passed me. It was my sport in those days to spot a party a long way ahead of me and set myself the challenge of not only catching them up but passing them. I would tick off groups of walkers as I passed and take pride in the fact that I was fitter than them. In other words, I was a prat.

Nature, or more specifically time, has now taken its revenge. The god of the hills has been watching and now everyone passes me. I tell myself that if I can just lose a little more weight or get out into the hills more, I will regain my fitness and put them to shame. This is a lie. It will never happen; I know that, and obviously the fit young folk who pass me on the climb this day also know that.

On this day on Ben More, something unusual happens. Within the first mile, I overtake a young couple who had been ahead of me. The young woman is urging her male companion on but he is struggling with the gradient. Before I can take too much pride in my minor triumph, I take a moment to reflect that there must be a reason why this young man is moving slowly. He is probably recovering from Covid-19 and the fact that he has risen from his sickbed to attempt the mountain at all means he has overcome insurmountable obstacles.

Far worse than the ignominy of being passed by younger people is the humiliation of being passed by older people. I'm in my late sixties. There is a tiny minority of folk who, while older than me, have the bad taste to still be much fitter than I am. Most of the people I know who are the same age rarely venture too far from the settee and spend hours happily discussing their many ailments.

There are, however, some folk who go around muttering things like, "Age is just a number". They are stick-thin and spend their days walking endlessly in the hills, giving even the youngest hiker a run for their money. These are fearless people who care nothing for the stereotypes of old age and will go through any barriers to pursue their love of the outdoors, like those eighty-year-olds who run marathons or lift 200 kilograms in the gym. They are all complete bastards because they give the majority of us, who live more typical lives, a bad name. They make it look like the vast majority of us are just not trying. We are the groaning majority. "Oh, my back/knee/ankles." Now that I've reached this age I can happily watch *Bargain Hunt* and sit enjoying tea and biscuits without feeling as if I really should be in the gym, doing forty sit-ups and drinking shakes made from turnips and leaves of jungle plants chopped up by a south American shaman. I know I should be fitter than I am but I comfort myself with the notion that at least I am here. I am sweating and puffing up this hill. You don't have to be in great shape. You don't have to put hours in at the gym. Just do what you can and enjoy it.

I am probably one of the last to arrive at the summit on this bizarrely hot April day. Even through the heat haze, the view is spectacular. I can see the patchwork of islands below me and the long peninsula of the Ross of Mull to the south, pointing the way to the holy island of Iona with its ruined abbey and ancient history. It is almost thirty years since I last gazed at this view but it has lost none of its magic.

Two hours later I am back in my tent. I have a wash, sit down in my chair, and watch the sun as it begins to descend. This is one of the great joys of hot tenting. I could stay here in a lightweight tent but the hot tent gives me room to move about and the space to sit in comfort. Perhaps it lacks the convenience of a campervan but it's a great base, and I'm as comfortable as I could be with the tent door open and the evening sun flooding in from across the sea.

The following day the weather remains good but my aching legs are pleading for a day off and I don't have the will to refuse. I spend the day lounging in the tent, reading and dozing. The time gives me an opportunity to reflect. Thirty years ago I raced up Ben More and was away on another walk the following day without giving it a second thought. Today my legs are stiff and I'd struggle to make it out of the car park. Now, however, I have something I didn't have before –the great gift of time. It is a Monday morning and I am sitting by this wonderful sea loch drinking tea. Thirty years ago I'd have been in an office counting the days to my next weekend of freedom. I don't have the legs I had back then, but I also don't have the pressures.

Above all, my hot tent has given me something you can't buy –it has given me freedom. I can turn any patch of grass into home. I can cope with any weather and move on as the notion takes me. Sitting in my tent, watching the sunlight dancing on the sea in this freakishly warm weather, I realise I have something beyond price. I have limitless freedom. That is what this hot tent means to me.

Chapter 25
Beginner's Guide

If you would like to have your own hot tent adventures, here are some hints and tips you might find useful. These are things that work for me but might not be right for you. One of the joys of this kind of camping is being able to adapt things to suit your needs. I hope you find this chapter useful.

What to Take

If you are new to hot tenting, it might be helpful if I give you an idea of the kind of things I take with me and have found useful. You will want to develop your own packing list that suits the sort of camping you do. I mostly go on solo camps, but you might not be a sad bastard like me and might want to take a partner, children or friends with you. If there are more than one or two people going, I'd suggest taking extra, smaller, tents with you so that folk have their own sleeping quarters. You can use the tipi as a social space where you can all keep warm, share meals and enjoy each other's company. Folk can then retire to their own lightweight tents to spend the night. In that way each person can spend the night without being kept awake by somebody's snoring or being stepped on when someone gets up in the night for a pee.

I wouldn't recommend trying to keep the stove burning all night. This may well be possible, although I have never tried it. My preference, no matter how cold it is, is to climb into a good-quality sleeping bag and let the stove go out. I've never been cold at night in my tent, despite being out in temperatures down to minus ten. I think it's pretty pointless trying to keep the stove going all night, as in order to stay alight it would need to be burning very slowly and so wouldn't give out enough heat to keep the tent warm –that's unless you can get someone keen enough to wake up every couple of hours and throw some logs on. If you have someone that gullible, then by all means let the stove burn overnight.

Tipi Packing List

Item	
Tent	I use a Tentipi Safir 7. I find it easily spacious enough for two or three people and all their kit. This tent comes in a smaller version, the Safir 5, or a larger version, the Safir 9. This is a single-skin tent. It is possible to buy an inner tent but I have not found the need of one, although it might be a good choice if you want a little additional comfort. The tent is completely waterproof and the heavy canvas flysheet is breathable. Provided you ventilate the tent

	properly, there is no problem with condensation. The Tentipi range –our giant hat Nordic kata event tipis and accessories
Pegs	The tent is supplied with its own pegs, as most tents are. I take additional pegs with me as spares.
Hammer	For knocking in pegs!
Floor	The Safir range of tents does not come with a sewn-in groundsheet. If you want a floor, you need to buy it separately. The floor fits neatly and securely, and attaches to the main tent by toggles. In Scottish conditions, I think a floor is essential. It will keep you dry and stop most of the wind from getting in. I would suggest pegging the groundsheet down using the pegs described below. This will prevent the wind getting underneath it and blowing the skirt of the tent out from underneath it. A floor will also give you some protection from insects which can be a plague in summer.
Pegs	I use Blue Diamond groundsheet pegs. These are short pegs, about four inches long. They have a flat plastic head which means if you stand on one, it won't damage the floor or injure you. I use these to pin down the walls of the tent and then I put the floor over the top to create a reasonably well-sealed living space. If I am camping on an area of thick grass, I sometimes use longer pegs so that I can get a secure anchor.
Cart	I often take a folding garden cart with me which is really helpful if you are camping any distance from your car. The cart enables you to move the

	tent and stove easily. If the ground is soft, very uneven or steep, hauling the cart can be hard work and it's difficult to haul the cart more than a few yards, but if you are travelling across firm ground or along a hard Land Rover track you can pull the cart some distance.
Woodburning Stove	I use a Tentipi Eldfell pro 7 wood-burning stove which is designed to fit the Safir 7 tent I own. I find it a little large for British conditions where temperatures are rarely very low, but it has never let me down and I find it great for cooking on. The tent is always warm. I have made two modifications to this stove. In order to better control the burn, I sealed the door with fire rope which is very easy to do. I also installed a damper (a rotating cast iron disc) in the chimney. In this way I can partially close down the exhaust gasses from the stove and make it burn slowly. The problem with all wood-burning stoves is that they have a tendency to produce too much heat, not too little. If you are setting up your own hot tent you might want to check out the range of stoves that are available on the market and try to find one that suits the conditions that you intend to use the stove in. For example, if you intend to camp exclusively in the warmer months a smaller stove might suit your needs. Whatever stove you use, you will need to ensure that it has a suitable heat displacement system where the chimney passes through the tent so that the canvas won't catch fire.

CO detector	I always take a small carbon monoxide detector with me and leave it switched on in the tent. The stove vents outside the tent and there should be very little chance of fumes coming into the tent from the stove. This is not the case with paraffin lamps and gas stoves which exhaust into the tent. Despite the tent being ventilated to some degree, even when the vents are closed, due to gaps around the floor, a CO detector is a good thing to have. CO is a silent killer. The detector costs less than fifteen pounds so there's no reason not to have one. My detector has never sounded in my tent but it is good to have it as a line of defence. At such small cost, I can see no reason why I wouldn't want to toss one of these little devices into my kit.
Firewood	It is important to use the right fuel. The best fuel is kiln-dried hardwood. Beware using unseasoned softwood. This will burn very poorly, give little heat and leave tar deposits in the chimney. There are lots of recycled products designed for wood-burning stoves available on the market. Most of these burn well. Do not use coal of any variety as you risk damaging the stove.
Axe	I carry a small wood-splitting axe so that I can make kindling if I need to or split logs if the ones I have are too big. I don't take a saw as I don't use fallen wood so I have no need to saw logs. I am no fan of the huge cult of outdoor knives that seems to exist. If you feel the need to make wood shavings that are easy to set fire to, then a sharp penknife is fine. I have never felt

	the need to carry some enormous Bowie knife that would take down a bear.
Matches	I live in perpetual fear of my matches getting damp and not being able to light a fire. Extra-long kitchen matches are great. For this reason, when I am camping or visiting a bothy I am always armed with several boxes of matches in a variety of plastic bags. On the basis that you can't be too careful, I also have a couple of cigarette lighters living permanently in the darkest recesses of my rucksack.
Stove for cooking	The Eldfell stove is great for cooking on, and it is one of the joys of hot tenting to be able to cook a fresh meal from scratch on a wood-burner. Although, if you just want a quick brew or you are making breakfast before heading out for the day, you may not want to go to the trouble of lighting the stove. In this case I find it helpful to have a couple of gas stoves on hand. There are some very good, cheap stoves on the market that sit in a square base and are very stable. These are not designed for backpacking but are great when you are camping with a car. These stoves are very easy to use and ideal for beginners. The shortfall of these stoves is that they run on butane which will not vaporise easily at low temperatures. If you are camping in colder weather, below five or six degrees (centigrade), then you'll need to take a camping stove that runs on a butane/propane mix. These are usually less stable. You could go the whole hog and take along a big double burner with a gas cylinder.

	The other possibility, for those of you who want to be really authentic and reproduce the Scott of the Antarctic vibe, is to get an old Primus stove that runs on paraffin. The old types of these stoves have become collectors' items and are not cheap to buy. Brand new versions of these stoves are available but again they are costly. It is also possible to buy petrol stoves. I have no experience of these so can't comment on them. Petrol is much more flammable than paraffin and can explode. Because petrol is risky, it is not something I'd want to carry about or have in a tent, but you may have different views.
Gas	For the camping stoves.
Pans	Pans with a heavy base conduct heat well and are efficient on the wood-burning stove.
Mug	
Kettle	
Sleeping bag	Once the stove is out it can be cold in the tent at night, so a good sleeping bag is essential.
Sleeping mat	There are a wide variety of mats available on the market. Some are simple foam mats and others are inflatable. The inflatable mats can be anything from £10 to £200. As weight is not a significant consideration with a hot tent, a cheaper but slightly heavier sleeping mat should be adequate. It's very important to be insulated from the ground in cold conditions. You might decide to go for one of the many folding beds that are available. With a folding bed you will still need some form of mat

	between you and the bed so you don't feel chilled by cold air circulating beneath the bed.
Spade	It is very important to be able to dispose of human waste properly when wild camping. I carry a garden spade which allows me to dig a deep hole and properly bury anything I leave.
Chair	I have a chair that folds flat which allows it to be stored easily.
Lamp	I'm very fond of my paraffin lamps. They give a great ambience to a tent. I am always glad to have one in the tent, not only for their light but also for the heat they give off. You can pick up a paraffin lamp for around forty pounds. I like the brass ones known as Duplex lamps. These have a double wick. The lamps are very simple so there is very little that can go wrong with them. Paraffin is also pretty safe in a tent and won't ignite in its liquid state unless it has a wick. The duplex lamps are very reliable, and will stay lit until they simply run out of paraffin. I purchase my lamps from Parrafinalia and enjoy polishing the brass until it gleams. I am a very sad person, I know!
Paraffin	Get the best quality paraffin you can.
Water container, large	I use a 10-litre water container which will carry enough water to last several days. In Scotland I'm very happy to use stream water. As long as the stream is running and is above habitation it should be safe. If I am going somewhere where I am uncertain of the water supply I will take some water with me.

Water container, small	The large capacity water container is heavy and cumbersome to use, so I always carry a water container of about a litre capacity which I fill from the larger water carrier.
Washing-up bowl	
Carpet	The great luxury that you can use in a hot tent is a carpet. This transforms the tent into somewhere that resembles a home from home. Initially I used a large piece of carpet which was fitted to the size of the tent. I found this to be too heavy to use so now use four or five smaller scrap pieces of carpet which are much easier to handle and cover the floor of the tent more than adequately.

Leave No Trace
As always, follow the Leave No Trace philosophy. If we all act responsibly then these wonderful sites will be available to all of us for many years to come.

There are seven principles to Leave No Trace:
1. Plan ahead and prepare
2. Travel and camp on durable surfaces
3. Dispose of waste properly
4. Leave what you find
5. Minimise campfire impacts
6. Respect wildlife
7. Be considerate of other visitors

It might help if I expanded on those principles a little. When I leave any campsite, I aim to ensure that the only thing I leave behind is an area of flattened grass where my tent stood. This will vanish in a few days as the grass recovers.

I always follow some simple rules, the most important of which relate to fires in the outdoors.

I never burn dead wood I find in the area and certainly wouldn't cut down any live wood. Dead wood –that is, fallen trees and branches –forms a very important environment for insects and invertebrates, so removing dead wood damages the environment. Cutting limbs from trees obviously damages them and is totally unacceptable. Live wood doesn't burn very well anyway. I bring any wood I intend to burn, usually in the form of kiln-dried hardwood. The woodland this is taken from will regenerate over time.

For some folk, camping and campfires seem to be synonymous. They can't camp without a fire. I can understand that having an outdoor fire has a social element to it and there is something primeval about lighting a fire in the outdoors. Sadly this means that it's not unusual to find the remains of campfires left by previous visitors who used the site years before, as scorched earth takes a long time to recover. I often demolish the rings of stones left by old campfires and try to find fresh soil to bury the area so that grass can return.

I've had debates on social media with many folk who enjoy wild camping and I have come to realise that there are some misconceptions about what Leave No Trace (LNT) means with regard to campfires. I've seen quite a few folk who consider themselves to be LNT campers but think it is perfectly fine to have a campfire as long as, when you leave, you ensure that the fire is out and bury any ash that remains. This effectively removes any evidence that there has been a fire, essentially hiding the damage.

My view is that this is not what the LNT camping philosophy means at all. LNT is about minimising the effect of our camping on the environment. That means not scorching the earth in the first place, rather than simply covering over the damage. Hiding the evidence is a bit like burying the body after a murder. It may be that no one can tell that a crime took place but the sad fact is that the victim is still dead. A fire made on the ground kills all the insect life beneath it and destroys all plant life. It can take years for the ground beneath a fire pit to regenerate.

One of my hobbies is to try to return areas of scorched earth to their previous state and I've found that this is much harder than I imagined. I demolished a circle of stones that surrounded an old burnt-out fire at my campsite in Kinloch Hourn by putting all the stones back in the river they had come from. I then took some turf from a riverbank that was about to collapse into the water and partly covered the blackened area with it. I returned to the spot seven months later expecting to see at least a little regrowth but was disappointed to find that not a single blade of grass had regenerated in half a year. I'm sure that in time the area will recover but suspect that it may take several years.

I'm sure some folk will argue that wildfires are a natural occurrence, and for some environments, they are an essential part of the life cycle. That is certainly true, but I think there is a difference between wildfires and a campfire. Most wildfires, at least the ones I've seen in Britain, are fairly short-lived and quick-moving affairs. A wildfire will sweep through an area, burning whatever fuel is available, and then move on. A campfire, on the other hand, is artificially created by folk bringing wood, or even coal, and then burning it in one spot for several hours. This creates a longer-lived and more intense fire that burns hotter and longer than a natural fire. As a result the heat penetrates further and does more damage than the average wildfire.

I have only had one encounter with a wildfire on the hills,

but it was spectacular. One warm May I spent the night in Corryhully bothy, an estate bothy that sits in the glen spanned by the viaduct made famous by the Harry Potter films. There I met a reserved gentleman who spoke with an educated Glaswegian accent. We sat together beside the fire in the sparsely furnished stone shelter and talked about our lives in the hills. Until we realised that we were both writers, the conversation turned to books.

The man I was talking to introduced himself as Ian Mitchell who, together with Dave Brown, wrote the classic hill book that inspired me to begin writing, *Mountain Days and Bothy Nights*. We spent the rest of the night talking about our literary adventures. I am glad we met this way. That's how it should be. We came together accidentally in a remote bothy, neither knowing who the other was. That's one of the magical things about bothies: you never know who you are going to meet and such encounters enrich our memories.

In the morning we went our separate ways. He was planning on climbing a hill whilst I was to walk across the hills to Glen Pean bothy in the next glen. We said our goodbyes and walked off in different directions. I have never met him since. The day was hot as I made the steep climb up over the high pass and began to descend towards the head of Loch Arkaig. As I descended, I smelled smoke in the air and became aware of a substantial fire a few hundred feet below me. At first, I reasoned that it was muirburn (the estate intentionally burning the old heather so new shoots could form to support livestock) and I should have no problem passing it.

As I drew closer to the flames, I realised that there was no one watching over it as there would be if it was muirburn. This was a true wildfire and completely out of control. I could see it advancing at about walking pace towards the path I was walking down to. The fire covered a big area but was confined to a narrow line of flames passing over the ground, consuming the dry grass and then moving on. I thought I could outrun it and get to the path first, but it was deceptive and barred my way before I could reach the path. Luckily I was close to a shallow rocky ravine where the fire could make no headway and I scrambled into there to wait for a few minutes until the flames passed by. Once it had moved on, the ground below me was blackened and smouldering but presented no difficulty. In the glen below I found the culprit. On a flat piece of grass there was a small ring of stones with the remains of a campfire. The grass around the fire was unburnt for about fifty metres. The fire must have been caused by a spark from the fire travelling in the wind and igniting the dry grass some distance away.

The previous night had been warm and there would have been no need for a fire. I'm guessing whoever lit it spent a fruitless time trying to extinguish the escaped flames, gave up and scarpered, leaving the whole hillside burning behind them –about as far from LNT as you can get. They must have made a sharp exit and prayed no one would catch them. I spent that evening in Glen Pean bothy watching the fire progress slowly across the hillside, filling the sky with dark grey smoke. The fire burnt for three days and must have covered an area of over six square miles, all the result of lighting an open fire in such tinder-dry conditions. The floor of the glen was covered in timber, the result of the forest being recently felled. Had the wind changed, I would have had to leave very quickly, and I doubt the bothy would have survived.

If you want to have a fire, there are ways to minimise its impact. Folding fire pits are available that keep the fire off the ground, usually by supporting it on some sort of mesh or grid. Another alternative is to make a mound fire, which is a fire set on a layer of earth about forty millimetres thick and sitting on a piece of cloth. When the fire is finished, you can remove the earth and cloth and leave the earth beneath untouched.

Chapter 26

Places to Camp

"Wild camping" just means camping anywhere that isn't an official campsite. One of the great joys of this is finding your own place to camp. This book isn't intended to be a guide to wild camping in the Highlands but if you are new to this kind of camping, especially if you don't know the Highlands, finding somewhere to camp can be tricky. Here are a few places to camp to get you started. Once you have a little experience, you'll be able to find lots of places yourself.

I have listed some of my favourite campsites although there are thousands more for you to discover. One principle I follow in summer is to seek places where there is likely to be a breeze, to give me some defence against the dreaded midges. Coastal campsites are good for this. In winter the opposite is true and I look for some shelter from the wind –below a cliff face, behind a hillock or amongst trees.

I always avoid camping within sight of houses and I also don't camp on farmland or where there is livestock. Sheep are not a problem, but cattle are often curious and may pass the day licking your tent or using your car as a scratching post, both of which are to be avoided. Be especially careful of all livestock if you have a dog, no matter how well behaved it is.

In winter, remember that some of the places I have suggested are on roads which run into the hills for several miles until they terminate. These roads are likely to be very quiet in winter, giving you a great feeling of solitude. In periods where snow may fall, these roads need to be treated with caution. If snow falls they may not be cleared for several days, if at all. They are very unlikely to be gritted. There is a very real possibility of being snowed in. In these days of climate change such conditions are not very common, but they do still occur so care is required. If you are uncertain the best policy is always to ask local folk for their advice –the Internet won't be of much use in situations like this. As they say in the Highlands ... go canny.

Glen Affric
OS Grid ref NH 235 251

This is a really scenic campsite on a small beach between an island and the loch shore. Surrounded by high hills and deep forest, it is an atmospheric place that has a great wilderness feel to it. Its position in the forest means it should be sheltered from the wind, although the fact that it is surrounded by high hills means that rain is never too far away in all but the driest conditions. In the summer you may have to share the site with other folk but in winter you'll almost certainly be the sole camper there. The glen is legendary for its midges in summer.

Be aware that, although the campsite is only a hundred

yards from the road, access to it is down a steep bank which can be difficult if you are carrying a heavy load. The bank is too steep to pull the cart down as I discovered when both I and the cart ended up, as my grandfather would have said, going arse over tit.

Glen Cannich
OS Grid ref NH 254 328

Runs parallel to Glen Affric but is much quieter than its better-known brother. The glen lacks a little of the grandeur of its neighbour but has a character all of its own. There is great walking here, although the glen is less frequented than Affric and the walking is often rougher with fewer tracks. This campsite is about a hundred yards from the road and close to the river. A great quiet spot where I saw an adder.

Loch Loyal
OS Grid ref NC 616 477

There are lots of places to camp on the shores of this remote northern loch. This is one of my favourite campsites. You can camp on the shore of the loch or on the other side of the road beside a very obvious ruined cottage. Some of the camping sites have chains across to stop campervan parking but that's no barrier to a hot tent.

This is a great place to go to avoid the NC500 hordes. Despite the roads around the coast of Sutherland being choked in summer, it's very quiet away from the tourist routes and pretty much deserted in winter.

Loch Hope
NC 462 475
Plenty of campsites here with some spectacular walking on your doorstep. You can camp within yards of the path up Ben Hope, and no one will bother you. In summer it's a good idea to camp in the more open spots of this glen as there is a large and often very active insect population.

Sheigra
OS Grid ref NC 184 603
Sheigra is a beach site run by the National Trust, not far from Kinlochbervie. Strictly speaking it's not a wild campsite; there's an honesty box for donations of five pounds per night. The only facilities are a very basic toilet block half a mile away up a steep hill. There is a standpipe for water outside the toilet block. As the only water available is from this standpipe some distance from the site, it's a good idea to make sure you have plenty of water before you arrive on site. You'll also need to take your rubbish out with you. This is a tent-only site so there should be no campervans or caravans.

You won't have this place to yourself but I like it because it doesn't have the feel of a commercial campsite. There are some nice walks accessible from here and you can walk to some fantastic beaches. A great place for kids.

Kinloch Horn

OS Grid ref NG 958 053

This is a great campsite at the end of a twenty-two mile cul-de-sac. You camp beside a small loch surrounded by steep-sided mountains. There is some great hillwalking to be had right from the door of your tent, and the walk to Barrisdale Bothy is one of the finest coastal walks in the Highlands. There is a small settlement just over a mile away with a handful of houses. There is, in theory, a café there, although it is being renovated at the time of writing and I've never seen it open. This area is very quiet even in summer. In winter you won't see anyone.

Mull

OS Grid ref NM 514 372

The Isle of Mull is a fantastic place to visit and the grassy meadows between the coast road and the shore of Loch na Keal offer some of the finest wild camping in Scotland. There is good walking as you are at the foot of Mull's highest mountain, Ben More. The coast offers fantastic scenery and there is abundant bird life to watch. Mull is famous for its sea eagles and there is every chance that you will catch sight of these magnificent birds. Take your binoculars with you. The soil is shallow so take extra pegs as it may be difficult to get a solid anchor in some places.

Torridon

OS Grid ref NH 013 636

Taagan is a basic site situated in the Beinne Eghie nature reserve and managed by Nature Scot. As such, it is not a true wild campsite and has a very basic toilet block. This is a good winter campsite. During the winter months the toilet block is shut as it freezes up, but there are clean and well-maintained toilets at the visitor centre less than a mile away. The site is free but there is no water in winter. Being within the National Nature Reserve, there is fantastic walking in the area with dramatic peaks which would satisfy anyone. **Do not use this site between May and September as the midges are fiends here.**

Melgarve

OS Grid ref NN 468 958

Not far from Newtonmore, the road to Melgarve winds its way through a very remote area and ends some nine or ten miles into the hills. There is a bothy and a house here, but that's all so there is plenty of opportunity to set up camp along this road. There is good walking although it can be a windy spot. Beware in winter, as there is high snowfall here and it would be very easy to get snowed in.

Should you find yourself in the far corner of a remote Scottish glen, watching the walls of your tent sway in the breeze and, sensing the chill of the evening, reach for your matches to light the stove. If these things happen and you spend the evening enjoying the warmth of a few burning logs watching the flame of your paraffin lamp dance; this little book will have achieved what it set out to do. May you find as much joy in these simple pleasures as I have done.

Printed in Great Britain
by Amazon

16510776R00180